Victoria

Photo Research by Dan Hawthorne
"Partners in Progress" by George E. Mortimore
Produced in cooperation with the Greater Victoria Civic
Archives Society

In Memory of Hector

Dec. 1986
Sadie

Beyond the Island

An Illustrated History of

Victoria

Peter A. Baskerville

To Fran, Ian, Leslie, and Danielle

Windsor Publications, Ltd.
Burlington, Ontario

Windsor Publications—History Books Division
Publisher: John M. Phillips
Editorial Director: Teri Davis Greenberg
Design Director: Alexander D'Anca

Staff for *Beyond the Island: An Illustrated History of Victoria*
Senior Editor: Julie Jaskol
Director, Corporate Biographies: Karen Story
Assistant Director, Corporate Biographies: Phyllis Gray
Editor, Corporate Biographies: Judy Hunter
Sales Representative, Corporate Biographies: Gordon Stuart McNish
Editorial Assistants: Kathy M. Brown, Laura Cordova, Marcie Goldstein, Marilyn Horn, Pam Juneman, Pat Pittman
Designer and Layout Artist: J.R. Vasquez

Honorary Advisory Committee

Windsor Publications and the Greater Victoria Civic Archives Society wish to thank the following people for their valuable assistance in the preparation of this book:

Pip Holmes
L.J. Wallace
Flos Prior
Helen Beirnes
T.G. Denny
Ted Balderson
Lloyd Davies
Ian Haddow

Contents

The beach at Beacon Hill Park has long been a favourite spot for Victorians to relax, picnic, stroll, or, as in this shot, paint. (VCA)

Acknowledgments

VIEW OF VICTORIA, VANCOUVER ISLAND.

Most cities have difficulty locating themselves in time and space. Victoria is no exception. That this is so may surprise a few who have and many who have not lived there. After all if any Canadian city has a clearly etched image it is Victoria: a bit of nineteenth-century England transplanted and nurtured on a unique slice of Canadian real estate where snow falls only rarely.

Much in Victoria's past, however, belies this lotus-like image. To understand better the evolving characteristics of the island city, this short book attempts to situate Victoria's development within the context of urban change in Canada as a whole. It does not aim to be comprehensive. Rather it hopes to excite interest, provoke discussion, and encourage further research. If it achieves any or all of these, the author will be satisfied.

The writer and picture researcher would like to thank the staff of the Victoria City Archives, Charlene Gregg, Jody Wegren, and Penny Seedhouse, who have, under extremely cramped and trying conditions and, lamentably, with only minimal financial support from the city itself, provided essential assistance during the research of the book. While all the staff of the Provincial Archives of British Columbia were invariably helpful, special thanks must go to Kathryn Bridge of the Visual Records Division and to Patrick Dunae for his interest and for his timely uncovering of little-known and rarely used source material. Julie Jaskol of Windsor Publications has performed needed and yeoman assistance. Annette Igra's timely enthusiasm kept the writer on track.

For her encouragement and for reading and commenting on parts of the book, the writer would like to thank his colleague, Pat Roy. It is only partly because of the loss of all those weekends that this book is dedicated to a special few.

Victoria's first Parliament buildings, known as the "Bird Cages," and the original James Bay Bridge are visible in this 1860 view from the Songhees Indian Reserve across the harbour. This view of the city by Herman Otto Tiedemann is dominated by the array of ships moored in front of Victoria's merchant houses. Courtesy, Provincial Archives of British Columbia (PABC)

The Company Town: Image and Reality

Before 1858 Victoria and the surrounding area were under the direct control of the Company of Adventurers of England, commonly known as the Hudson's Bay Company. Because of this corporation's prominence on the northwest coast, the emergence of Victoria as a town has rarely received much direct attention. Rather, it is often assumed that Hudson's Bay Company policies precluded colonization and settlement, and thus, Victoria, to the extent that it grew at all, consisted simply of retired and often cantankerous fur traders.

As with most caricatures, this interpretation takes part of Victoria's reality and blows it up to represent the whole. In fact, Victoria in the pre-1858 gold rush era evolved into a town of surprising complexity. By adding flesh to the prevailing caricature, Victoria's image can be remoulded and the city's history can be better understood.

For the first third of the nineteenth century, European fur traders operating on the west coast of North America had all but ignored southeastern Vancouver Island.

The quest for the sea otter led traders to the northern reaches of the Pacific Ocean and the need for locally grown food drew them to the southern plain-like regions of the Columbia River basin. By the mid-1830s, however, pressures emerged which caused the Hudson's Bay Company, by that time the dominant fur trading corporation on the coast, to move its central depot from the Columbia River to a northern area more readily accessible by sea and, if possible, of equivalent agricultural potential.

The wreckage of Hudson's Bay boats on the sand bar at the Columbia's mouth in 1829 and again in 1830 provided part of the impetus for looking north; a continuing diplomatic dispute between Great Britain and the United States provided the rest. Who would ultimately control what was then the jointly occupied northwest coastal zone? From the Hudson's Bay Company's perspective, a central depot had to be situated in British territory. Could the company expect to hold at bay American settlers in a rich agricultural region? The "Little Em-

Sarah Crease, daughter of Victoria judge Sir Henry Crease, painted this 1860 view of the inside of the Hudson's Bay Company fort. Fort Victoria was established in 1843 as the western bastion of the huge fur trading company. By 1864 the fort was considered unnecessary and it was demolished. The area where it stood houses Victoria's central business district. (PABC)

Above: *This view of the sun setting over the island is from Haro Strait, east of the Saanich Peninsula. Photo by Bob Garlick*

Facing page, top: *One of the first depictions of Fort Victoria and its Indian neighbours, this Paul Kane painting is copied from a watercolour originally done about 1847 during one of his trips among the natives of present-day western Canada and northwest United States. The Indian village on the right is the original Victoria site; by the end of the nineteenth century the village was moved twice to allow the city's expansion. Courtesy, Royal Ontario Museum*

Facing page, bottom: *This view of Victoria in the late 1850s by Sarah Crease looks north from the government buildings across the James Bay Bridge to the city. The large building on the left is the Hudson's Bay Company warehouse while the spire in the background belongs to Victoria District Church. To the left and below the church is what remained of the Hudson's Bay Company fort in the late 1850s. It was completely removed by 1864. (PABC)*

peror," Sir George Simpson, governor of the Hudson's Bay Company in British North America, thought not. Worried by the influx of "worthless and lawless characters of every description from the United States" and suspicious of Great Britain's willingness to withstand American pressure, he "prepared for the worst" and in 1842 ordered the establishment of another depot "with the least possible delay" on the southern tip of Vancouver Island.

Accordingly, Chief Factor James Douglas, who had spent twenty-four of his forty years in the fur trade, reconnoitered the area and reported on the "decided superiority of Camosack . . . as a place of settlement." Its climate, harbour, prairie land, and relative accessibility to fresh water seemed to put it ahead of any other bay in the vicinity. In what was to become a common refrain, Douglas could not help comparing the area favourably with England "corresponding [as they did] in . . . insular situation and geographical position." With fifteen men, Douglas returned in March 1843 and commenced construction of Fort Victoria, officially named in June, after the reigning Queen.

Simpson's vision of the future of this "depot of the coast" foreshadowed the dilemmas that constrained and underlay Victoria's early development. Sensitive to the winds of change that were sweeping the area, Simpson realized that the company had to broaden its operations, concentrating less on fur and more on agriculture, lumbering, salmon fishing, and whaling. He hoped the new depot would play a central part in all these endeavours.

Yet the movement north occurred at a time of re-

trenchment and belt-tightening within the corporation. Victoria's commencement paralleled the closure of three other northwest depots. The capital necessary to underwrite the activities Simpson desired was not forthcoming. Fort Victoria would, after an initial settling-in period, be staffed with an absolute minimum number of employees. Nor were settlers, even retiring Hudson's Bay Company employees from the other side of the mountains, to be encouraged to settle as agriculturists. Conceived within a context of retrenchment and retreat, Fort Victoria's future seemed ambiguous indeed.

That the fort developed at all largely owes to the active support of the people upon whose lands it was erected. Although the Songhees Indians of southeastern Vancouver Island had only fleeting direct contact with Europeans before the 1830s, two sorts of indirect contact had proven extremely lethal. As early as the 1780s smallpox had swept the area, decimating the native population. Between that time and the 1830s guns had been introduced to northern Vancouver Island tribes and much bloodshed followed. By the early 1840s approximately 2,000 Indians remained in the southern areas with maybe one-half of these in the immediate vicinity of the site selected for Fort Victoria.

Simpson had feared that "a very large population of daring, fierce, and treacherous Indians" would cause the new depot much trouble. In fact, the reverse was the case. Douglas' diary indicates that the Songhees assisted the settlers in clearing land, building the fort, unloading and loading cargo, sounding the harbour, and procuring food (salmon and potatoes).

Why did the Songhees provide this assistance? Permanent European settlement enhanced the local natives' opportunity for stable and, from their point of view, lu-

Above: Fort Victoria was the center of the Hudson's Bay Company's northwest empire and until the early 1860s, one symbol of that empire. While other buildings appear in this photo, the fort originally housed all white residents of Victoria. (PABC)

Facing page, far left: The "Little Emperor," Sir George Simpson, was the governor of the Hudson's Bay Company in North America at the time of Fort Victoria's founding. He chose Victoria as the site for the company's westernmost post, the focus of a vast commercial empire as well as a bastion of British imperialism on the Pacific. (PABC)

Facing page, left: James Douglas was the major force in the early development of both Victoria and the province of British Columbia. He served as chief factor for the Hudson's Bay Company, governor of the Crown Colony of Vancouver Island, and from 1858 to 1863, chief executive of the fledgling mainland colony of British Columbia. (PABC)

crative trade. The blankets and ammunition which they received for their labours, while cheap from the company's perspective, were sought by the Indians. It is also probable that they looked on the Europeans as potential allies in their battles with northern tribes. The Songhees had already constructed forts to withstand northern attacks at nearby Cadboro Bay and Esquimalt Harbour.

VICTORIA

Left, above: *The bridge connects the city to the southern James Bay area as shown in this 1860 painting by Edmund Thomas Coleman. The red buildings on the far shore are the province's first Parliament buildings. Today, the area to the left of the bridge is landfill, and houses the prestigious Empress Hotel. (PABC)*

Left: *The Flying Squadron lies at anchor in Esquimalt Harbour around 1870. Esquimalt Harbour housed the Royal Navy contingent as well as most large ships on commercial stops. The arrival of the Flying Squadron was always a celebrated event in Victoria. This painting is by Scottish surgeon Alexander Rattray. (PABC)*

The mountains of what is today Washington's Olympic Peninsula provide the backdrop for this 1863 view of the "Bird Cages," built in 1859. The local paper described the buildings' architecture as something between a Dutch toy and a Chinese pagoda and they soon acquired their nickname. The wooded area behind them became one of the city's most fashionable neighbourhoods by the 1880s. (PABC)

Above: *This sketch, looking south down Government Street, illustrates how the bastion dominated the early townsite. In the distance can be seen the natural growth of the James Bay area against the backdrop provided by the mountains of Washington's Olympic Peninsula. (PABC)*

Facing page: *The "Flying Squadron" docked regularly at Esquimalt, unable to enter the too-shallow city harbour. Provisioning the fleet was big business for local merchants and the Hudson's Bay Company especially benefitted from this. The dock in the foreground in fact belonged to the company. (PABC)*

Not surprisingly, then, when Fort Victoria was completed, numerous Songhees (Douglas estimated 700 in 1850) abandoned their traditional winter sites and formed at least two villages cheek to jowl by the fort. From this position they could both protect and be protected by their new trading ally.

Between 1843 and 1849 Fort Victoria gradually consolidated its position as the center of the Hudson's Bay Company's northwest operations. By 1847, 300 acres produced 1,000 bushels of wheat, 400 bushels of peas, 700 bushels of oats, and 3,000 bushels of potatoes. The original fort was extended 135 feet to the north (its northeast corner stood at present-day Government and Fort streets) and a "Commodious cowhouse" and sizable warehouse were erected outside the fort.

Victoria's development took on even greater significance in January 1849 when the British government, hoping to forestall American expansion, granted the Hudson's Bay Company formal control of Vancouver Island. In return for this the company paid seven shillings a year for ten years, agreed to attract significant British settlement in five years, and promised to set aside nine-tenths of all land sales for the colony's general development. By December 1854, according to a census compiled by Douglas, 232 people lived in the town of Victoria, about two-fifths of whom were under the age of twenty. The town itself contained seventy-nine residences, twelve stores and shops, and twenty-one out-

houses. By early 1858 a few more dwellings had been added, and the population, according to most sources, had apparently peaked at roughly 300.

Small wonder that many historians have concluded that the Hudson's Bay Company failed to fulfill its bargain. Similarly it is generally conceded that Victoria in this period was at best a "respectable English village," a "tranquil little hamlet," and less kindly, "an outpost community of small endeavours and limited opportunity."

Unfortunately these tidy little epitaphs tend to obscure as much as they enlighten. There are three reasons why this period in Victoria's history deserves more than passing mention. In the first place the causes of this growth rate were not transitory. In many ways they set the contours of Victoria's future. Secondly Victoria's long-term role as an entrepot was refined and entrenched in this era. And finally, without an understanding of the principles underlying the emergence of Victoria's town plan—a plan that, according to its creator, surveyor Joseph Despard Pemberton, stood the test of time—subsequent events such as the impact of the Fraser River gold rush in 1858 and the emergence of the incorporated city in 1862 cannot be properly assessed.

It is too simple to claim, as many have, that the Hudson's Bay Company concentrated on fur trading and discouraged all other aspects of colonial development. As we have seen, Simpson, the company's governor, argued strongly for broadening the company's economic base.

Coal mining, lumbering, fishing, and agriculture assumed an increasingly important role in the firm's general operations. Direct trade in fur at Fort Victoria was rarely of much importance; in 1844 the depot collected only 400 beaver and land otter skins. Rather, during this era Victoria's function as a general trading entrepot became clearly defined.

As in so many other aspects of Victoria's early history Indians played a crucial role in trade. Victoria quickly became a focal point for annual trade migrations by Indians. Salmon, shingles (manufactured by natives), fur, potatoes, and cranberries were traded for blankets, ammunition, and other items. Victoria then exported many of these goods to a diverse network of trading allies.

Many of the links established in this period continued for the rest of the century. In 1846, five Royal Navy vessels stopped for supplies, thus commencing a relationship that lasted for nearly sixty years and proved to be of great importance to Victoria's economic well-being. Trade in foodstuffs with the Russian-based fur trading concern, the Russian-American Company, in Alaska, presaged Victoria's role as an entrepot in the mid-1860s after the United States purchased Alaska and again in the late 1890s during the Klondike gold rush. The export of goods to San Francisco and the Sandwich Islands proved to be significant. Victoria shipped out salmon, coal, lumber, and shingles.

From the Sandwich Islands, Victoria received sugar

and molasses for general trading purposes and salt for preserving salmon. Of equal importance, Victoria also imported Kanakas from the Sandwich Islands as general laborers both for local employment and for use throughout the company's coastal depots.

Most significantly, the Hudson's Bay Company expected the area to provide supplies for its own fur traders and to act as the transshipment point for all fur to England and for all English trading goods to the interior. In doing so Victoria commenced a nearly fifty-year role as window to the world for British and ultimately Canadian possessions in the Northwest.

Several more or less enduring factors, however, severely hampered these various initiatives. The viability of Victoria's role as an entrepot depended on the demand for products available to it. In this period and in later years the demand fluctuated dramatically, and Victoria, whether as a fort, townsite, or city, could do little

to control it. Because of high American tariffs, San Francisco, for example, was a rich market only in the early 1850s when a local gold rush created a high demand and high price for lumber and foodstuffs. Exports to San Francisco declined following the end of that gold rush in 1853. Similarly trade in fur with England, despite the Hudson's Bay Company's virtual monopoly, depended on the vagaries of style (beaver hats were increasingly out of fashion) and on the conservation of a rapidly depleting fur stock on the western coast.

Even assuming the existence of supply and demand, Victorians had to contend with several local constraints. From a merchant trading perspective, Victoria's harbour possessed serious limitations. Two Royal Engineers reported in 1846 that the entrance, because of a sand spit extending off of Shoal Point, was "rather intricate." A special report in 1862 warned that even vessels drawing only fifteen feet "encounter delay as well as risk of grounding." Moreover, an extensive bed of rocks within the harbour made loading and unloading space along wharves very limited. The 1862 Victoria Harbour Commission established by the colonial government put the cost of constructing, operating, and maintaining a "steam dredge" to render the harbour more accessible at $69,000 for the first year. When completed in 1864, the machine cost a reported $90,000 and two years later was "lying idle, having been tested and condemned as useless."

Technology and capital could ultimately overcome the harbour's deficiencies. The agricultural potential of Victoria's immediate hinterland was a more intractable problem. Despite the hopes of Simpson and Douglas, the possibility of southeastern Vancouver Island providing adequate produce for the general fur trade, the Royal Navy, the Russian-American Company, and local consumption was remote. Readily available arable land simply did not exist. As George Colquhon Grant, the first colonist independent of the Hudson's Bay Company, put it, the island was "little better than a mass of Rock, with a few little garden patches as it were, interspersed at intervals along the seacoast."

Douglas, who became head of the fort in 1849, also realized that bringing even the best land under cultivation required hard labour and much sacrifice. He estimated that three years' work would be necessary before a farm could become a profitable enterprise. Given the immense distance by sea from England, the high wages and prospects of gold in California, the nearly free grants of land available in Oregon following 1850, the high tariff which restricted trade with the United States, and the roughly 50 percent increase in the cost of living in Victoria compared to England, attracting and keeping both company employees and independent settlers was a formidable task.

The Hudson's Bay Company responded to this challenge in two ways. Acting through Douglas, they "negotiated" a series of what were known as Fort Victoria treaties with the various Indian tribes on Vancouver Island. In the spring of 1850, for the sum of approximately $555, the Indians of the Victoria district signed a blank sheet of paper on which Douglas later transcribed "the contract or Deed of conveyance" which ceded their land

to the British government. The Songhees were allowed to live on a reserve across the harbour from the fort, and after 1855 on a second and smaller reserve on Esquimalt Harbour.

Drawing on the most widely accepted principles of colonizing practice, the company then instructed Douglas and the resident surveyor, J.D. Pemberton, to prepare a town plan and general structure for colonization. These principles dictated that land should be kept at a cost that would discourage "squatters, paupers, and land speculators" and encourage that which "is most valuable and most approved" in existing British society. Founded on a rigidly hierarchical division of labour, the company wished to transpose the similarly structured traditional class divisions of England to Victoria and Vancouver Island.

Working within this general frame, Pemberton attempted to achieve two further objectives: concentrate settlement within the town of Victoria, and encourage the development of farming in its immediate hinterland. He instituted a three-tier system: town lots of roughly 60 feet by 120 feet would sell for fifty dollars; suburban lots of five acres would sell for $125; and country lots of at least twenty acres would sell for five dollars an acre. His plan would, he believed, lead to concentrated settlement within the town and allow for ordered and controlled expansion as population dictated. He hoped to avoid what he described as the "slovenly pultroons" created by Oregon's town plans which seemed to permit wide dispersion and ruinous speculation. In his town plan he also provided for a large park area (the origin of Beacon Hill Park), a reserve for schools, an allotment for churches, and the preservation of stands of trees both for their beauty and for protection from winds whipping across the Strait of Juan de Fuca.

In order to encourage farming, Pemberton and Douglas successfully advised the company to grant twenty acres to retiring servants on condition of settlement; to allow for instalment payments; and, although it is not clear that the company formally agreed to this, to permit allowances for rock and swamp when charging for country lots.

The town plan instituted by Pemberton, while employing a very typical grid structure, nevertheless represented an innovative, controlled, and surprisingly egalitarian approach to urban development. His attempt to stimulate focused urban growth while providing for the development of an agricultural hinterland was, without direct acknowledgment, recognized in 1918 when Thomas Adams, a famous British town planner, praised Victoria as "one of the finest cities of its size on this continent." In particular Adams noted how well integrated the city was

By the 1860s Esquimalt Harbour housed extensive warehousing facilities, reflecting its role in the shipping of goods through Victoria. Later, Esquimalt became home to the largest drydock facility on the west coast of Canada and to Canada's maritime fleet. (PABC)

with its surrounding agricultural belt and how, compared with other western cities, it had escaped "the sterilization of its suburban lands by excessive subdivisions." Pemberton would have been pleased.

If in the long term Victoria and its surroundings evolved as Pemberton had hoped, what of the short term? Recent research by Richard Mackie at the University of Victoria has revealed that between 1849 and April 25, 1858 (the arrival date of the first boatload of prospective gold miners), seventy-two people purchased 132 town lots in Victoria. Only twelve bought suburban lots and 109 acquired 17,536 acres in country lots. This distribution was quite compatible with Pemberton's design. As Pemberton had hoped, suburban lots appealed to only a "limited class of purchasers." Population was relatively concentrated in the town and in its agricultural hinterland. Space remained for planned expansion.

The general colonization model within which Pemberton worked posited that land should be of a price sufficient to create a labour pool to work the estates of large landowners. Over the course of a few years these labourers would then have accumulated enough resources to acquire and work their own relatively smaller lots of land. Within this hierarchical structure, the area would thus develop in a balanced and stable manner. Pemberton's refinements did not alter the model's overall intent. His refinements did, however, determine the differing characteristics of the population of the town and of the country.

Pemberton's programme permitted significant diversity in terms of the town landowners' occupational and ethnic backgrounds. Fully one-half of the purchasers of town lots were or had been labourers in the employ of the Hudson's Bay Company. Because the company paid its labourers about eighty-five dollars a year plus room and board, it seems clear that the institution of the instalment plan helped make it possible for this class to own land in Victoria.

In terms of ethnic background, too, the social mix of town dwellers was more varied than the caricature of retired British Hudson's Bay Company traders would lead one to believe. Only thirty-five of the landowners had been born in England or Scotland. Most of those remaining were Kanakas from the Sandwich Islands and French Canadians from Lower Canada. Since the Kanakas and French Canadians were generally labourers, it seems likely that their numbers would be increased by those in the town who did not own land. Unfortunately there is no census to which one can refer for a definitive statement.

Nevertheless it is interesting to note that in December 1854, only thirty-one of 108 males over the age of twenty owned land in the town. Two speculations might be hazarded from this evidence. If we assume that 30 percent of adult males owned land in early 1858—i.e., that the proportion of landowners to landless remained roughly the same—then some 170 did not and most of these were probably Kanakas or French Canadians, i.e., labourers. Therefore, the majority of Victoria's population was of other than English and Scottish heritage.

Such an assumption would also lead to a second conclusion: that the total population in the town, often stated as 300, is somewhat of an understatement when women and children are added to the seventy-two male landowners and 170 non-landowners. Given that women and children represented over 50 percent of the population in 1854, then a figure in excess of 500 would seem to be a more reasonable estimate of Victoria's population on the eve of the 1858 gold rush. This figure, while small, takes on more significance when it is realized that Victoria represented the largest concentration of non-natives in British territory west of Red River and surpassed any settlement in neighbouring Washington Territory.

To a degree, the town's institutions reflected its social divisions. Churches catered to varied clientele; both Anglican and Roman Catholic places of worship were established in this period. In early 1849 Douglas founded a school suitable for children of the upper ranks of the Hudson's Bay Company employees. An Anglican minister, Robert Staines, assisted by his wife, took over the position of teacher and chaplain. Six months later a school for Roman Catholic children commenced under Father Honoree Timothy Lemprit. In 1852 Douglas, worried that the children "of the labouring or poorer classes" were "growing up in ignorance, and the utter neglect of all their duties to God and Society," established a common school children could attend for four dollars a year. In addition to these official institutions several private schools, including one for girls, opened before 1858.

Like schooling, general social activities reflected Victoria's class divisions. Little social interaction occurred between classes. The company's officers ate, slept, and played separately from the company's servants. Only visiting officers of the Royal Navy vessels were admitted to their dinners, balls, theatre groups, and other social festivities. At times, as in October 1855, a forbidding "Grand Theatrical Opera" was "celebrated" at the Naval Hospital in Esquimalt—there being no regular theatre. At other times theatrical plays and balls were held on whichever of His Majesty's schooners happened to be in the harbour. Lieutenant Richard Charles Mayne, visiting Victoria in 1855, commented how "In fine weather, riding parties of the gentlemen and ladies of the place

were formed, and we returned generally to a high tea, or dinner tea, at Mr. Douglas' or Mr Work's [an HBC chief trader], winding up the pleasant evening with dance and song."

While Douglas' son-in-law, Dr. John S. Helmcken, a long-time Hudson's Bay Company employee and the fort's official doctor, could state with satisfaction that "the few very few upper ten" set the tone and pace of Victoria's society, this comment ignores the lives of the majority of the town's inhabitants. As a result the social routine of the company's servants is very difficult to re-create. We do know, however, that residential distinctions, even at this early date, were so marked that the Kanakas lived in what was called Kanaka Row (modern day Humboldt Street). Ownership of a town lot certainly did not bring with it social acceptance by the Hudson's Bay Company elite.

Nor did this ownership permit direct involvement in the colony's political affairs. At this time the town of Victoria possessed no local government; rather, along with the rest of the colony until 1856, it was ruled by an appointed council, handpicked by James Douglas. The council members were all top-level Hudson's Bay Company officers, some of whom were related through marriage, thus giving birth to the term "family-company-compact." Under some pressure from the few non-Hudson's Bay Company residents and from the British Colonial Office, Douglas constituted an assembly in 1856 to which seven members were elected.

To vote, however, one had to own at least twenty acres of freehold property and this effectively barred the franchise from almost all Victoria's residents. No member officially represented the town, although three members represented the district within which Victoria was situated. Not surprisingly, those elected (who had themselves to own 300 acres or $1,500 of immovable property) continued to reflect the upper echelons of the company's

The building of the Colonial School gave the children of "the labouring or poorer classes" opportunity for an education. Like many nineteenth-century political leaders, James Douglas was committed to at least rudimentary social, moral, and academic education for all white children. (PABC)

administration.

Pressure to enfranchise the town resulted in the passage of a bill by the assembly in June 1857. This legislation granted Victoria two members to be elected by men who owned town property including improvements worth at least $250. The council, however—which had also to pass all legislation in the colony—deferred examining the bill until March 1859. It took another eight months of wrangling before the council reluctantly assented, as they put it, "simply on the grounds of expediency." Even then they did so within the context of a bill which increased the total number of members from seven to thirteen—obviously in the hopes of diluting the town's political power.

This delay reflected the different interests of town and hinterland residents. Before 1858 there was very little overlap between the two; only thirteen of 109 country landowners also owned land in the town of Victoria. One council member worried during a debate on the enfranchisement bill that the passage of the act would give to the town "a preponderating influence in the House of Assembly, and the country generally might find itself taxed to carry into affect [sic] town improvements." True to its design, Pemberton's land holding system had led to a distinct split in personnel and class between town and country. The tensions inherent in these differences came increasingly to the fore in the years following the 1858 gold rush.

The Gold Town: Plus ça Change, Plus C'est la Même Chose

People commonly presume that the discovery of gold on the Fraser River in 1857 through 1858, and in the Cariboo in the 1860s, had a shattering effect on Victoria's development. Certainly the influx into the town of some 25,000 "varied specimens of humanity" from San Francisco in the summer of 1858 could not help but change the town's physical site, general living conditions, and collective psychology.

Yet a broader view is necessary. On the eve of the discoveries, settlement was increasing in Victoria's immediate hinterland; land sales exceeded those of 1856 by three times. Moreover, as Douglas pointed out in his 1857 annual report, because "of an increased demand for Coal and Sawn Timber in the markets of the neighboring countries," business "speculations" were rising. The gold rush occurred at a moment of upward prosperity. This underscores an often overlooked point: Victoria existed as a viable entity before the gold rush. Finding gold may have led to the parallel discovery of Victoria, but it did not mark the occasion of its birth.

If Victoria predated the gold rush, it also survived it. At a number of levels the gold rush was a transitory phenomenon. Most of the initial 25,000 or so arrivals in 1858 simply disembarked, provisioned, and moved on as quickly as possible to seek fortunes panning gold on mainland rivers. During the winter of 1858-1859, the majority of these passed back through; disgruntled, impoverished, and often dependent on public charity for survival. Some stayed, hoping to profit as merchant middlemen, transportation agents, land speculators, general handymen, and providers of various consumer services. Between 1858 and 1863 Victoria's year-round population fluctuated between 3,000 and 6,000. In most winters, miners returning from the goldfields added to these figures. Following 1863, as easily available gold became scarce, Victoria's population declined to around 1,500, rising slowly to 5,925 in 1881.

In some cases, then, the gold rush accelerated preexisting economic, political, and social trends; in others it fostered new developments. By 1880, from this coalesc-

CHAPTER II

One historian has concluded that the "Bird Cages" attested to "the new prosperity of the colony." Certainly they attested to an odd combination of architectural styles which inspired their nickname, one that remained with them until their demolition in the 1890s. (PABC)

Above: *The gold rush of 1858 sparked interest in Victoria in England. The London Illustrated News ran a full-page sketch of the burgeoning community as well as a lengthy article. The* News *assured its readers that "there is no finer site for a city in the world" though the "life is very primitive" for most of the gold seekers. (PABC)*

Facing page: *The Victoria Hotel was the first brick building in the city, erected in the gold rush year of 1858. This 1890s shot captures the building much as it was, with a name change the biggest difference. The advent of brick as a building material was a benchmark in the city's development. (PABC)*

ing of new influences and old patterns, a city with increasingly well-defined if not all together attractive social, political, and economic attributes had emerged.

The Hudson's Bay Company's relationship to Victoria nicely illustrates the notion of continuity amidst change. An investigation of the company's role in general mercantile and land policy sheds much light on the nature of Victoria's development in these years. Before 1858 the company enjoyed a legal monopoly of trade with all natives on Vancouver Island and the interior and, given its size, a *de facto* monopoly of trade with other inhabitants. Company personnel dominated the colony's government and controlled its economic and social transactions. Yet even before the discovery of gold, signs existed which foreshadowed an end to this era of formal dominance. An 1857 Select Committee of the British House of Commons severely criticized the company's overall operation. Old company leaders were retiring and new outlooks were emerging. Its twenty-one-year trading monopoly was due to expire in 1859, and few believed it would be renewed. In this context the gold rush acted as a catalyst for the removal of the company from control in the Pacific Northwest.

Formal relationships and overt symbols were quickly erased. Late in 1858 Douglas quit the company's employ

and became the Crown's representative not only for Vancouver Island (he had been representing both the Crown and the company there since 1851) but also for the whole of the mainland. A proclamation from the Queen ended the company's trading monopoly in 1859. The company's fort began to be dismantled in 1860—the northeast bastion at the corner of View and Government was torn down in the winter of that year with the rest of the fort suffering a similar fate in 1864. Now hotels, churches, mercantile houses, banks, and the first Parliament buildings—the "Birdcages"—began to dominate the fast-expanding townsite.

Mercantile and transportation competition swiftly emerged. By 1860 the town boasted twenty grocery stores, thirteen dry goods shops, seven hardware operations, and most significantly, thirteen commission merchants. The latter group, which had more than doubled by 1863, competed directly with the Hudson's Bay Company for the lucrative trade with miners on the mainland. The company also lost its control of the carrying

trade as American and, increasingly, colonial-built boats vied for passenger and merchant traffic.

If the gold rush facilitated the opening of what had been primarily the Hudson's Bay Company's personal preserve, it did not alter the trading pattern that the company had fostered. If the scale of operations changed dramatically—$1,156,880 of imports landed at Victoria between July 1 and September 30, 1858, and the previous yearly high had only been $65,000 in 1853—Victoria's traditional role did not. By declaring Esquimalt and Victoria free ports in early 1860, Douglas merely extended a pre-existing policy. By denying free port stature to any other center, Douglas preserved the island town's domination of mainland trade. In addition to this status, Douglas had already, in 1858, designated Victoria as the sole spot for the sale of mining licenses. Consequently, all miners had to touch at the island port before proceeding to the mainland.

Given this economic context, it is not surprising that merchants, especially those involved in the import-export

The import-export dimension of Victoria's early economy cannot be overemphasized. It was the lifeblood of the city. S.J. Pitts was one of the leaders of this commercial clique, as the size of his establishment suggests. (PABC)

sector, came to dominate Victoria's internal leadership. The Chamber of Commerce, founded in 1863, had as its first president Robert Burnaby, an import-export merchant. James Lowe, with ties to the Hudson's Bay Company, was also prominent in the chamber's early affairs. Similarly, import-export merchants formed a disproportionate number of those elected to Victoria's early city councils.

The policy of this mercantile elite, however, tended to be narrow, unimaginative, and in certain ways slowed Victoria's development. If free port status benefited the merchants, it is not clear that other Victoria residents enjoyed similar gains. Despite the absence of tariffs, the cost of living exceeded that in Great Britain by 100 percent. Along with merchants, those with marketable trades could increase the cost of their services accordingly. Government appointees, residents on fixed incomes, and the growing number of unemployed miners could not.

The merchants' main plank, the continuance of free port status, blocked the emergence of an autonomous municipal structure in Victoria. In the first place merchants were beholden to James Douglas for the implementation of this policy. Douglas, while sympathetic to merchant needs, also respected the fears of country dwellers that Victoria must not be allowed to dominate the colony's affairs. As a result incorporation bills dragged slowly through the legislative process in the early 1860s. Reluctant to criticize Douglas too severely, Victoria's merchants dragged their heels. Not until August 1862 did Victoria achieve incorporation as a city and even then all local by-laws had to receive the governor's assent before they could be implemented.

Even more fundamentally, the incorporation bill did not clearly grant to the new city any independent power to collect revenue. In part this again reflects the power of country over town in this period. It also reflects the simple fact that without customs revenue the colony of Vancouver Island had to rely on other money to run its affairs. Trading licenses, land taxes, and land sales formed the bulk of these alternative sources. Following 1863, revenue increasingly fell short of expenditure and the city quickly fell into arrears to contractors and other city employees.

Clearly the colony required some new means of raising capital. Yet Victoria's merchants remained intransigent. When the mainland colony of British Columbia and Vancouver Island decided to merge in 1866 in order to economize on administrative costs, the city's merchants waged a losing battle against the imposition of tariffs, the loss of free port status, and the designation of its rival New Westminster as the new capital. Thanks in part to pressure from the Hudson's Bay Company, Victoria regained the status as capital in 1868. Even more significantly, a scant year after the institution of the new revenue system, the legislature amended Victoria's charter and granted the city some independent power to collect money for local needs.

Not until the abrogation of free port status could the city of Victoria begin to emerge as an independent entity. The local merchants failed to realize that and only slowly adjusted to the new environment. In 1867 and again in 1869 many—but far from all, and generally non-British—merchants signed annexation petitions in the hopes that by joining the United States they could reestablish free trade status. A similar fragmentation of the mercantile community occurred over the issue of Confederation.

In the midst of this despondency, however, some local merchants and financiers, young and generally of British origin, gradually came to the fore. Edgar Crow Baker, an Englishman, Robert Patterson Rithet, a Scotsman, and William Curtis Ward, a British-born financier and manager of the Bank of British Columbia from 1866-1896, best typify this group. These men slowly adapted to the new realities and by the end of the 1870s stood

Victoria's first mayor, Thomas Harris, is reputed to have tipped the scales at over 300 pounds and to have smashed the mayor's chair the first time he sat in it. He ruled over the initial city council before retiring to pursue his various business interests. (PABC)

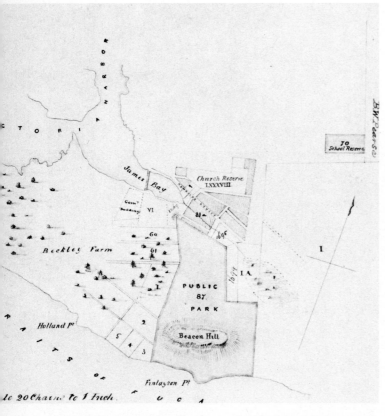

Above: *This map illustrates the areas originally allocated by Pemberton as church, public park, and public school reserves. It is believed that this map was drawn according to the original specifications during the HBC land-selling controversy in an attempt to clarify the situation. (PABC)*

Facing page: *Construction of the customs house relieved in a small way the impact of the 1870s depression as well as providing a new home for government agents. It still stands today, in a form virtually unaltered from this circa 1875 photo. (PABC)*

poised to lead and profit from the economic resurgence of the next two decades. Their collective activities marked the commencement of a new era in Victoria's history.

Through the Hudson's Bay Company's control of the town's land site, the company helped determine the pattern and tempo of Victoria's physical growth. The 1849 agreement with the British government had given the company the right to sell all land on Vancouver Island. Nine-tenths of the returns had to be used to develop the colony's infrastructure; one-tenth went for the Hudson's Bay Company's private use. With the expiration of the agreement in 1859 many felt that the company would have nothing further to do with land sales on the island and in particular with land sales within the fast-expanding townsite of Victoria. The company argued differently. It claimed that 3,084 acres had been set aside for its personal use before the agreement was reached with the British government and that the agreement did not cover the reserved acreage. It so happened that this acreage included the townsite of Victoria and the greater portion of the adjoining suburban lands. During the gold rush these lands commanded inflated prices, and the directors of the Hudson's Bay Company determined to profit from their sale.

Before 1859, sales of Victoria land had been generally overseen by Douglas in his dual role of governor of Vancouver Island and representative of the Hudson's Bay Company. Douglas argued that while he controlled these sales, speculators were checked and no one person was allowed to purchase more than six lots. Donald Fraser, member of the Executive Council, correspondent for the London *Times,* and a chief propagandist for Victoria in England, concurred. In his January 1859 column he asserted that "In no case of any other new town do I know of so many small proprietors who own their own houses on their own land. Victoria is emphatically a town laid out for the benefit of the poor man."

That this was true even in 1859 is doubtful. It was emphatically not the case under the policy followed by the Hudson's Bay Company between February 1859 and January 1862 when the choicest of the remaining lots were disposed of at a series of private sales that netted the company in excess of $300,000. None of this money was taxed and none of it went toward the maintenance or expansion of the town's infrastructure. Ten percent of the buyers purchased over 50 percent of the lots. The top five purchasers obtained over one-quarter of the lots sold and four of those men were currently or had recently been top Hudson's Bay Company executives. The fifth was none other than Fraser.

In the course of selling this land the company ignored

the official town maps drawn up by Pemberton and, according to the disgruntled surveyor, "sold and continue to sell what Lands they thought or think proper, including portions of the Public Park Reserves, the Church Reserve, the Indian Reserve, the Public Wharf Reserve South of the Fort etc." Perhaps most galling and indicative of the company's desire to squeeze all the benefit it could from the current situation was the sale of the ornamental oak trees within the town limits for firewood—trees, which Pemberton explained, "I was strictly ordered by His Excellency to preserve. . . ."

The Hudson's Bay Company disposed of this varied property at a time when its legal claim to it was under dispute. When the colonial secretary in England became fully cognizant of the situation and ordered the company

to cease selling pending a resolution of the conflicting claims, the company had already sold most of the best lots in Victoria. A final resolution not only upheld the company's rights to the land in question but also recognized its ownership of significant quantities of suburban real estate north and east of Victoria. This guaranteed that the company would have an ongoing influence in Victoria's growth.

Only a few could afford to speculate in the land market. The majority of those who bought land in Victoria did so to live on it. These lots generally were not in a "desirable" business or residential area, but they were relatively cheap in an era of inflated prices. Of the speculators, we know that the Hudson's Bay Company profited nicely and returned none of that profit to the

Above: *The construction of city hall in 1877 was an indication of the optimism civic leaders still retained for their city. Victoria's fate as the second city in British Columbia was yet to be sealed by the awarding of the national railroad terminus to Vancouver, and Victoria's leaders still dreamed of a future as grand as the new city hall. (PABC)*

Facing page: *Victoria's active maritime industry supported many ship chandlers. Merchants such as E.B. Marvin profited from both commercial vessels and Her Majesty's Royal Navy, a frequent visitor to the city. (PABC)*

city. As for the fate of individual speculators, the available data is too fragmentary for a precise answer. This much seems clear: those who profited from land sales did so before the assessment of November 11, 1863. Following this, Victoria's economy and population began a dramatic decline with a significant turnaround not transpiring until the early 1880s.

Little residential or business construction occurred between 1864 and the mid-1870s. Some institutional building provided work for the ailing construction trades following 1875. Yet the commercial core, bounded by Johnson, Douglas, Wharf, and Fort streets, remained virtually untouched after the mid-1860s. Although the city contained about 1,500 buildings in 1863, less than one-third of all purchased lots contained improvements. By 1871 the assessed value of property and improvements owned by individuals had declined 60 percent from its peak in 1863. Donald Fraser continued to own the most lots, having disposed of only eighteen in the in-

tervening eight years. As late as 1881, close to one in three of Victoria's residences were vacant.

Relatively little economic activity occurred outside the areas of mining, land, and trade. Gold mining declined precipitously after 1863. A find near Victoria in August of that year provided some excitement but proved too small—only $75,000 was taken out in 1866, "hardly paying grub" for the miners involved—to offset the lack of mainland discoveries.

As gold declined, so did Victoria. "We are Commercially as dull as ditch water," the Bank of British Columbia's manager reported in January 1865. "Skedaddling and bankruptcies alone are lively." The principal business of those merchants who remained in Victoria was supplying Indians and the local whites, and perhaps most significantly, catering to the needs of the sailors from Her Majesty's Royal Navy when their boats docked at the nearby Esquimalt port. An informed observer estimated that in this way the Royal Navy brought some $400,000 to $500,000 of business to Victoria each year.

Manufacturing in the form of baking, brewing, distilling, and gas production had emerged by the mid-1860s. From a long-term perspective, however, the most significant diversification occurred in the areas of shipbuilding and general iron and steel work. By 1864 two foundries and machine shops employed roughly 100 employees at what seems to have been the going wage for skilled labour: five to six dollars per day. During 1865 a third foundry and boiler manufactory commenced operations. Only one—the Albion Iron Works owned and operated by Englishman Joseph Spratt from San Francisco—remained active in 1866. Even it, according to the Bank of British Columbia records, was in severe financial straits. With the advent of Confederation in 1871 and the prom-

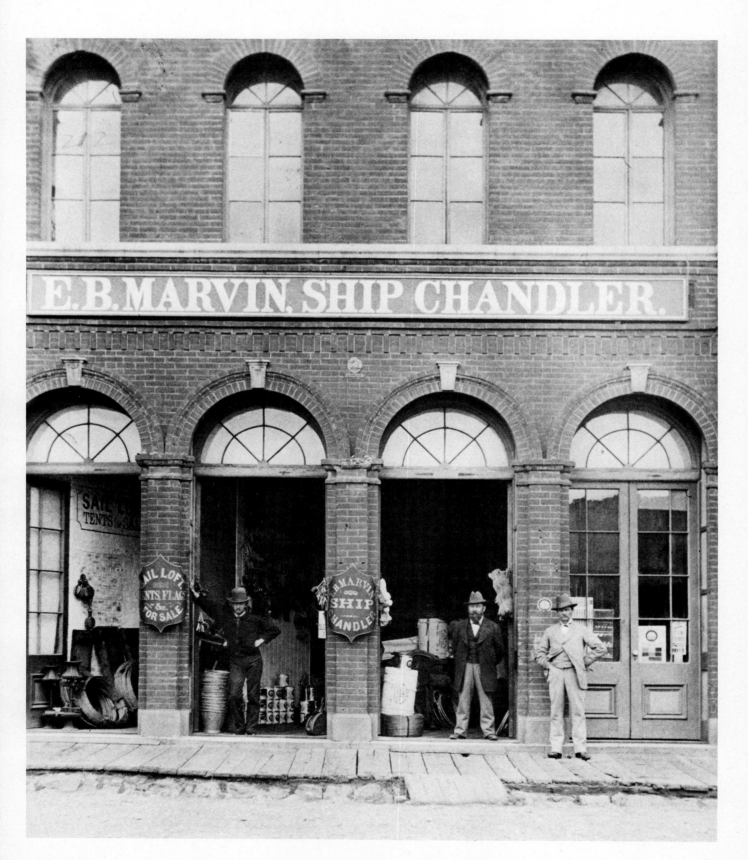

ise of a transcontinental railroad ending at Esquimalt, business at Spratt's foundry picked up. By the mid-1870s he employed some sixty men and had a monthly payroll of $4,000. At the same time he diversified his operation and established the Victoria Machinery Depot for the construction of cargo steamships to transport Vancouver Island coal to markets in Seattle and San Francisco. Indeed, between 1867 and 1879, 41 percent of all new tonnage registered in British Columbia was owned by residents of Victoria. Clearly, a shipbuilding and general iron and steel industry that served mines, sawmills, ships, and assorted city needs took root in Victoria in these years. Sustained activity in this sector would, in the future, belie Victoria's image as a simple entrepot for merchants and haven for tourists.

It is tempting to characterize Victoria in this period as simply an extension or outpost of San Francisco. American influence did bulk large. One informed observer stated that in 1862 "nearly half of the commercial business of Victoria is in the hands of Americans" and that these merchants had some $500,000 capital invested in the city. The American mercantile influence, however, like the gold rush itself, proved to be transitory. With several important exceptions (William Parsons Sayward and C.C. Pendergast for example), most American entrepreneurs left Victoria following the decline of the gold rush and the end of the Civil War. By 1881 only 12 percent of Victoria's population was American-born.

The term "outpost" of course implies more than national overlap; it generally refers to a dependent relationship. A quick glance at trading statistics in this period certainly lends support to such a contention. For much of the 1860s about 50 percent of all foodstuffs consumed in Victoria and the mainland were imported from Washington, Oregon, and California. Hardware and assorted trading goods swelled the American import list. With the exception of gold, relatively little was exported to the United States.

By the later 1860s and throughout the 1870s, however, there is evidence to suggest that a significant percentage of the nonagricultural products imported from the United States had themselves been shipped in bond to San Francisco from Great Britain for re-export to Victoria. The American consul at Victoria reported that nearly one-half of all imports from the United States fell

Albion Iron Works was the largest foundry on the West Coast north of San Francisco. Its rise and fall, its owners, and its close connections to the seagoing trade may, in large part, symbolize Victoria's late nineteenth-century economy. (PABC)

VICTORIA

The Bank of Columbia established itself in Victoria in 1862. It was a major financier of nineteenth-century city development. The government also financed its operations partly through the bank. The stability of the Bank of North America and the Bank of British Columbia contrasted with the transient nature of some other financial institutions that dotted the city. (PABC)

in that category and that about two-thirds of all exports to the United States were for transshipment to Great Britain. This suggests that Victoria was not simply a trading appendage to San Francisco; rather, San Francisco was to a surprising extent simply a middleman between Victoria, the British Northwest, and Great Britain.

The British presence was equally marked in the financial sphere. In 1859 the British-headquartered Bank of British North America established a branch in Victoria and in 1862, in addition to several private banking firms, the newly incorporated London-based Bank of British Columbia commenced operations. It opened a branch in

San Francisco in 1864 and throughout the nineteenth century underwrote the American-British wheat trade, and general trade and development in the Victoria area. Fragmentary evidence from the 1860s suggests that the Bank of British Columbia took funds out of Victoria as the local economy began to decline, thus restricting local credit and forcing many merchants who had become accustomed to extended repayment periods to file for bankruptcy. In a financial as well as economic sense, Victoria may indeed have been an outpost of Great Britain, not San Francisco.

In other ways, Victoria was far from a simple mirror image of "merry old England." Even before the gold rush, ethnic diversity characterized Victoria's population. The gold rush further accentuated this fact. One historian has commented that "few towns in the entire world claimed such cosmopolitanism." People came, generally via San Francisco, from such diverse countries as Poland, France, Austria, Spain, Italy, Switzerland, Germany, Holland, Denmark, Sweden, Russia, the West Indies, China, Mexico, Chile, Malaya, the Sandwich Islands, and, of course, Great Britain. This ethnic diversity led to a proliferation of national clubs, benevolent societies, and religious centers. The Scots, English, Germans, and French formed benevolent societies to protect the welfare of their respective ethnic groups. In the early years of the gold rush the French community even published a French-language newspaper. The Americans formed their own chapter of the masonic order to rival one already founded by the British. The first *Victoria Directory* in 1860 listed over a dozen Jewish-owned business ventures and by 1863 this significant community had constructed its own synagogue. By the same date there were also two Anglican, one Roman Catholic, one Wesleyan, one Congregational, and one Presbyterian church serving Victoria's varied religious needs.

A hierarchical social structure cut across this ethnic and religious diversity. Those of Scottish birth founded two benevolent societies: St. Andrews, in 1858, composed of well-to-do merchants, Hudson's Bay Company officers, and government officials; and the Caledonian Benevolent Society, in 1863, composed of a wider range of traders and businessmen independent of the Hudson's Bay Company and the government. Each conducted its own social and benevolent activities and each marched separately in the various festive parades—like that held on Queen Victoria's birthday—so typical of this period. The pattern of social visiting on New Year's Day, 1866, aptly symbolized the nature of Victoria's social hierarchy. The British visited the governor and the American consul; the "city elite" enjoyed a luncheon given by Mayer Selim Franklin, a Jewish merchant, in honour of

Christ Church Cathedral was the focus of the establishment Anglican church. This is the second Christ Church, built in the early 1870s to replace the first, which was destroyed by fire. Later in the century a third Christ Church replaced this wooden structure and still serves Victoria today. (VCA)

Above: *This dour group was in pursuit of Victoria's favourite pastime. These men were likely to have been members of the city's elite because cricket seems to have been strictly an upper-class pursuit. (PABC)*

Facing page: *While 25,000 gold seekers poured into Victoria in the rush of 1858 the town retained at least remnants of its proper British heritage. Cricket matches were a popular event as early as the 1860s and were later joined by such "aristocratic" pursuits as sculling and horse racing. (PABC)*

former Mayor Thomas Harris and members of the city council.

A review of Protestant church membership suggests that occupational status combined with ethnic background to influence religious persuasion. Small retailers, mechanics, and lesser tradesmen attended the Methodist, the Congregationalist, and the Scottish Presbyterian churches. Bankers, lawyers, large wholesale dealers, Hudson's Bay Company officials, and government appointees attended the establishment Church of England.

Private denominational schools dominated Victoria's educational system and instilled in the minds of the elite's children the "proper" values of society: obedience, as Douglas remarked in 1852, to "God's Society." What happened to those who could not afford to attend? Victoria, in common with many other nineteenth-century

North American cities, had increasingly to confront the perceived problem of "street Arabs," "children," as the local paper, the *British Colonist*, put it, "of the poorer classes . . . running about the streets in idleness and consequent mischief." Situated outside the city limits, the one government-supported school was too far away for children too poor to attend private schools. In 1869 the government decreed that local municipal councils would act as school boards and raise money for local education. The city council failed abysmally in this task. The two common school teachers, having worked eighteen months for just six months' salary, went on strike in September 1870. Continual pressure from citizens, educators, and the local newspaper finally resulted in the passage of the Public School Act of 1872.

Under provincial jurisdiction public schools reemerged in Victoria. Although nominally non-sectarian, in reality this system encouraged the teaching of Protestant prayers, the Ten Commandments, and the King James version of the Bible. In this way the government believed

that the teachers could best "innoculate" the "highest morality" into their lower-class students. With the passage of compulsory attendance laws in 1873 for all children aged seven to fourteen, a system for the maintenance of class stability was in place.

Public entertainment exhibited a similar class basis. Rowing, horse racing, and cricket occupied the elite. The first and second concerts of the Victoria Philharmonic Society in June 1859 took place before a select audience headed by the governor's party and, as one local confided to his diary, "all the nobs." Officers of the Royal Navy and members of the Victoria Amateur Drama Club regularly entertained the governor and his entourage, highlighting Shakespearean drama such as *Othello* and *Hamlet*. Such cultural events took place in surroundings "fitted up in elegant style, with Parquette & Pit . . . cushioned seats, . . . chandeliers" and, in the case of the Royal Theatre, its owners promised "that on no consideration will Indians be admitted." Nor were blacks welcomed other than in the cheap seats, the gal-

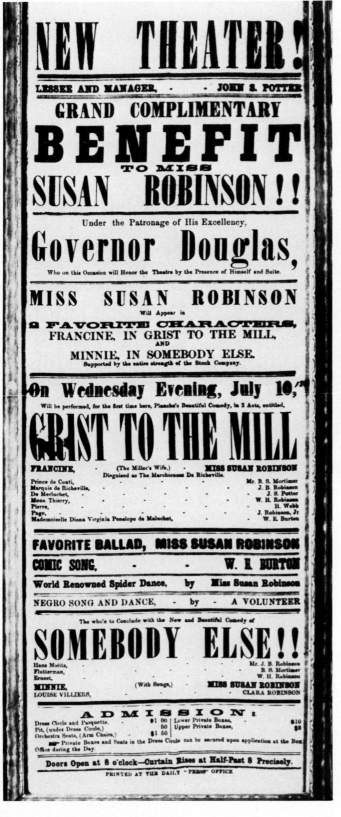

Above: *The flip side of the apparent propensity of early Victorians to drink was the temperance movement active in the city. These people are posed in front of the Angel Hotel, an aptly named temperance enterprise. (VCA)*

Left: *The "proper" values of society might very well have included an appreciation of the theatre. Victoria was the host to stage productions from its infancy as this 1863 bill confirms. (PABC)*

lery. For those who could not classify as "nobs," however, there was another option. A second regular theatre "of much lower standards," the New Idea, presented "Sentimental and Comic Singing: Negro Minstrelsy: Laughable Farces" with a new show nightly. These festivities took place, in somewhat less opulent surroundings, under a local butcher's shop.

For Victorians not interested in formal musical and theatrical presentations there were other diversions. Despite Douglas' pronouncement that liquor was "the prolific source of poverty and crime," he granted twenty-three retail and eight wholesale liquor licenses—including one of the latter to the Hudson's Bay Company—in July and August 1858. By 1866 his successor, Governor Arthur Edward Kennedy, reported that eighty-five "*licenced* public houses for the retail of drink and some twenty additional wholesale or gallon houses" existed in Victoria. Members of the elite, like Attorney General Henry Crease, lamented in 1870 that:

Night houses or hotels are kept open without restrictions as to hours or persons and boys from ten years old allowed to drink and play cards at them with impunity— terrible glimpses of the way in which the youth of Vancouver are being brought up.

Nor did these alternative diversions stop at drinking and cards. While the charge books of the city police do not reflect a high incidence of prostitution, several other indicators suggest that this was a thriving business in Victoria. The local constabulary complained in August 1865 to the colonial secretary that some 200 Indian prostitutes lived "in filthy shanties owned by Chinese and rented . . . at four to five dollars a month" in the area of Cormorant and Fisguard streets. No "respectable" person could walk in that district even by day, let alone at night when "scenes . . . of drunkenness and rioting" were such that "a dozen of police could not keep order or decency." His solution—Victoria's standard an-

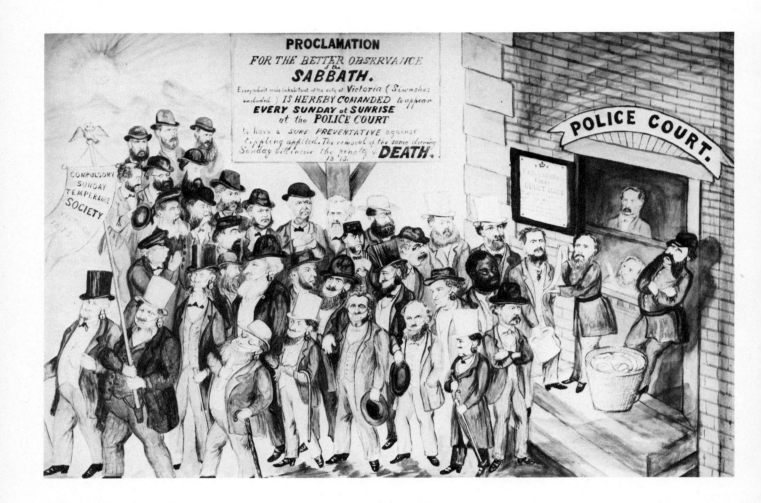

swer—was to run the Indians out of town and keep them on the reservation. The extent of prostitution in Victoria is also suggested by the significant incidence of venereal disease amongst Victoria's residents. Hospital records for various years in the 1860s and 1870s reveal that roughly 20 percent of those admitted suffered from such maladies as "fungus of the testicle," syphilis, syphilitic rheumatism, and gonorrhea. The records also reveal that only a minority of these were sailors—by far the majority lived, worked, and played in the city.

To keep such "play" within acceptable and peaceful bounds Victoria appointed a full-time constable as early as 1854. Four years later, Augustus F. Pemberton established a regular police force along the lines of the London Metropolitan Police system. High transiency, significant graft, and, for a few dedicated officers, excessive overwork at little pay, characterized its operations. A sampling of police charge books for 1859 and 1862 reveals that two-thirds of all charges concerned "victimless" crimes with slightly under one-third concerned with

Above: *Separate from the police, Victoria possessed its own militia to protect the city from attack. The uniforms of these men were purchased, ironically, from their only possible enemies, the Americans. A Seattle group had purchased them, found them unsuitable, and resold them. (PABC)*

Facing page, top: *This 1873 cartoon mocked both the temperance movement and the general population. The sign is exhorting every adult male to appear at the police court each Sunday to receive a sure preventative against "tippling." (PABC)*

Facing page, bottom: *Victoria constructed an imposing stone gaol in 1862. While drunk and disorderly conduct was the most common sentence, it did not receive the stiffest penalty. Harsher punishment was reserved for those refusing duty on domestic ships, those who enticed sailors to desert Her Majesty's service, and for general military-related charges. This reflects well Victoria's concern for creating a reputation as a safe and orderly port in order to attract military and general foreign trade. (PABC)*

crimes against persons and property. One in three charges related to drunk and disorderly conduct.

The high rate of drunk charges may simply reflect the relative ease with which drunkards, as opposed to thieves, could be apprehended by an understaffed and ill-equipped police force. Nevertheless the overall pattern of arrests tends to reflect the pre-industrial nature of the town. Petty thievery, loose morals, drunkenness, and minor property violations loomed large in other developing pre-industrial North American urban centres as well as Victoria.

Certainly the high proportion of single males to single females characteristic of such towns was particularly marked in Victoria during the gold rush. One contemporary estimated that in the mid-1860s there were 100 males for every female in the city. When in 1862 the Emigration Society in England, at the request of Reverend Edward Cridge, the colony's second Anglican chaplain, sent over a boatload of single women, the city proclaimed a spontaneous holiday and the wharves were crowded with eager bachelors waiting to appraise the new arrivals. As late as 1881, males between the ages of

twenty-two and forty-six outnumbered females of that age by some 30 percent. This sexual imbalance encouraged prostitution, drinking, and rowdiness.

The high transiency rate associated with such centres was also particularly marked in Victoria. Few came to stay. Miners provisioned and left. Northern Indians traded and left. Most merchants stayed only as long as business seemed buoyant. To maintain law and order within this context of high population turnover, the attorney general of British Columbia felt that Victoria's finest:

should not be interfered with in the practice hitherto pursued by them of making arrests without a Warrant as delinquents would almost certainly escape if the strict rule were followed.

Scattered evidence suggests that this and other *sub rosa* procedures were employed especially rigorously in the case of presumed Indian and Chinese offenders. Local county court judge A.F. Pemberton complained in 1880, "there are so many [of them] roaming about day and

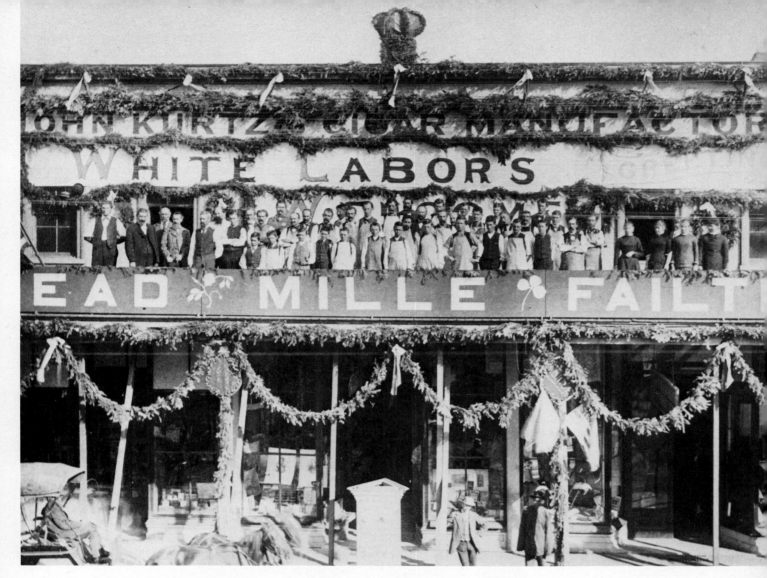

night an expeditious mode of punishment is much needed," and recommended "summary jurisdiction" as an acceptable remedy. He added that the local courts were "happy to cooperate with His Worship the Mayor and Municipal Council in effecting the removal of Indians from within the City Limits."

After conviction, Victoria's prisoners suffered a fate which, with the later exception of Vancouver, does not seem to have been common in Canadian cities. They became working members of Victoria's "chain gang." Throughout this period anywhere from thirteen to twenty convicts, "heavily chained," worked five and one-half days a week "carrying out," according to Victoria's senior convict guard, "important public works." This provided the city with relatively cheap labour for road work, sanitation removal, and general construction.

During and following the gold rush the new Victorians did not, as had the Hudson's Bay Company before them, desire to interact with natives on a respectable economic or social level. The new wave of Victoria residents perceived the Indians not as co-workers but as a threat. Referring to the roughly 2,000 Indians camped in and near Victoria in 1860, the *British Colonist* argued strongly against their employment by white settlers: "It is Caucasian-Anglo-Saxon bone, muscle, and intellect that

Above: *John Kurtz's cigarmakers extended "white labor's" greeting to the Marquis of Lorne in 1882. As in other established crafts in other centers, the Victoria cigarmakers represented a nativist approach to non-white labour. The Oriental worker was perceived to be a threat to their well-being. (PABC)*

Facing page: *The few people who did come to Victoria to stay established the basis of a residential neighbourhood east of the city in 1872. This photo, taken from Christ Church Cathedral, emphasizes the impact of Pemberton's grid system. (PABC)*

we want." As the historian Robin Fisher has written, "The Fur Trade . . . stimulated Indian culture by adding to Indian wealth and therefore to the scope of Indian creativity. Settlement—often [subtracted] from Indian wealth and thus tended to stultify their culture." Certainly this was the case with respect to the Indians in and near Victoria.

While there were exceptions, most Victorians regarded the Indian in one or a combination of three ways: as a sexual object—one settler confided that "Among the Females there is a *painful* and *provoking* scarcity of petticoats"; as consumers of cheap whiskey—alcohol diluted with salt water and flavoured with brandy, rum, whiskey, camphine, creosote, "and even sulphuric acid"—sold by, among others, Hudson's Bay Company employees; and finally, as purveyors of filth and disease. In December 1862 the city council passed a by-law "to take measures for improving the Sanitary conditions of the City of Victoria . . ." which simply made it unlawful for Indian women to live inside city limits unless they were registered as servants.

Outbreaks of smallpox in 1862, 1868, 1875, and 1876 became the occasion for "rounding up" and "driving off" all the Indians city authorities could find. Applying for money from the provincial government to carry out these evictions in 1876, the city council admitted that "at this inclement season of the year [late November] it would look as though we were inhuman to do so but the health of the Citizens must be preserved. . . ." The council gave no consideration to the federal Indian commissioner's suggestions that the Indians be quarantined and vaccinated rather than sent away to spread the disease elsewhere. Nor did the council attempt in any concerted way to take action to prevent future outbreaks. In their minds, as in the minds of most Victorians, the area's original inhabitants were "savages," not "citizens." Social harmony necessitated the expulsion, not the integration, of "non-Caucasians."

A second non-Anglo-Saxon group suffered somewhat less harshly at the hands of Victoria's white leaders. By the early 1860s some 600 blacks had moved north in an attempt to escape the slavery and racism so rampant in the United States. They received a mixed welcome. Those who arrived early purchased land at a relatively cheap price and a few, like Mifflen Wistar Gibbs, became successful merchants. Gibbs even sat on Victoria's city council in the early 1860s. Most remained at lower occupational levels. For several months in 1859 Douglas appointed black men to the police force, but American miners would have none of it and the appointees were soon dismissed. Others volunteered for fire department duty, but white volunteers withdrew their services.

Blacks formed a Pioneer Rifle Corps; however, when a white corps was founded several years later, not only were blacks refused admission, but the black corps was also denied the right to march in the official ceremonies marking Governor Kennedy's accession to power in 1864. The reason was simply that since they were the first corps in existence, had they marched, they would have done so in front of all other corps. Victoria's white riflemen would not stand for that.

And so it went. Some churches (Reverend Cridge's Anglican Church) would accept black parishioners; others (Reverend Macfie's Congregational Church) established a "nigger's corner." Some saloons permitted integration; others refused to serve "former slaves" or charged them exorbitant prices. Under pressure from the parents of white children, the sisters in charge of the Roman Catholic girls' school put "the Coloured children" in a separate room. Despite a riot by blacks at the city's major theatre in November 1860, seating areas remained restricted throughout the decade. By the late 1860s it hardly mattered. Most blacks had either returned south or moved elsewhere, often to Salt Spring Island in British Columbia. An anonymous black reporter writing on "The Coloured Inhabitants of Vancouver Island" for the *Liberator*, an anti-slavery journal published in Boston, concluded in 1864 that "Prejudice is too strong in Vancouver Island."

Initially, a third "non-Caucasian" group found a ready welcome in Victoria. Some 4,000 Chinese arrived en route to the goldfields in 1860 and the *British Colonist* remarked on what a boon they were for the merchants, especially in the sale of hardware and big boots. A minority set up residence in the island town. By 1862 eleven Chinese companies paid a trade license tax and Kwong Lee's import-export firm was second only to the Hudson's Bay Company in the size of its assessment. As gold petered out, many Chinese moved to Victoria to become small merchants selling to other Chinese, providers of services to the general white population, or servants and cooks employed by Victoria's white elite. By the close of the 1870s, of some 2,000 Chinese residing in British Columbia's capital, approximately 400 were employed in domestic service.

The patronizing attitude of the elite towards their Chinese servants is suggested in the following excerpt from a letter written in 1864 by Sarah Crease, the wife of an up-and-coming Victoria lawyer:

We have all been longing to let you know what a charming Chinaman we have got I don't know when we have had things so comfortable as since he came. He is clean, orderly and industrious, bakes and cooks to our hearts

Left: *The Hudson's Bay Company and other companies early learned the advantage of Chinese labour. While this man's task is unknown, his presence on an HBC horse serves as a perfect illustration of his role in early British Columbian society as a labourer for large economic concerns. (VCA)*

Below: *While the "Chinee" asks "why you send me offee?" the reply from Victoria's member of Parliament is "because you can't or won't assimilate with us." In 1879 the M.P., Amor De Cosmos, supported a petition requesting the prohibition of Chinese labour in railway work. (PABC)*

content and (what we feared about) washing the clothes quite as well as Sarah at her best. . . . God, I'm sure sends such Chinamen as all good things come from Him.

As early as 1865, however, many of Victoria's white population began to regard the Chinese less as economic assets and more as competitors and impediments. The first anti-Chinese riot in British Columbia took place on Victoria's docks in that year. Chinese were increasingly perceived to be pimps and slum landlords living in filth and producing disease. By the late 1870s provincial legislation, strongly supported by the *British Colonist,* threatened to levy special taxes on Chinese workers and employers. In 1879 Victoria's merchants, calling themselves the "Workingmen's Protective Association," urged city council to exact a prohibitive licence on all peddlers, "almost exclusively . . . Chinese," in order to protect "retail stores in the City."

Unlike the blacks, the Chinese did not leave. Rather, in 1872 and again in 1878 many Chinese domestics, labourers, laundrymen, and peddlers withdrew their services in protest against unfair discrimination. This strike activity suggests that during the 1870s a strong Chinese community emerged determined to protect and where possible extend Chinese rights within their adopted town. It was not enough that the Chinese, like the Kanakas before them, lived physically apart from the general white population. Their resistance and persistence was more than most white Victorians could abide. A petition signed by Mayor John H. Turner and Victoria's city councillors in February 1880 appealed to the government to restrict further immigration of "Mongolians, most of them slaves." This was only the beginning of a determined effort on the part of the city to protect what it considered to be its proper self-image and destiny from the "evil" contamination of yet another alien, non-white group.

The Emerging Metropolis: Growth and Identity

Ranked by population, Victoria was only the twenty-seventh largest Canadian city in 1881. Hoping the city would become the terminus of the Canadian Pacific Railway (CPR), as promised in the early 1870s, Victorians shuffled their feet "waiting," as one local realtor put it, "to see what our friends east of the Rocky Mountains intend to do." Immediate prospects seemed dismal. "An air of discouragement . . . pervades the whole city," Allen Francis, the American consul, informed his secretary of state in July 1881. "Numberless dwelling houses and many eligible stores formerly occupied and showing life and activity are tenantless." The city's physical state reflected and reinforced the general despondent atmosphere. "Day by day the dusty streets are swept by the breeze; to the infinite discomfort of the dweller and the visitor," complained one observer. "Night by night the noxious gases of their primitive road side gutters are disinfected [only] by the cool draft from the mountains."

This lethargic beginning gave no clue to the fact that in the 1880s Victoria would experience greater expansion than in any other decade in its history. Its population increased by 184 percent—the second highest growth rate of any Canadian city in that decade. This made Victoria the eleventh largest Canadian city by population. Its physical site doubled to seven and one-half square miles. Reflecting its continued control of the region's trade, imports doubled and exports increased by one-third. At the same time significant economic diversification occurred. Gross value of manufacturing production increased 3.5 times. And, incredibly, when ranked by per capita value of manufacturing production, Victoria stood fifth out of the twenty Canadian towns and cities with a population in excess of 10,000.

By 1891 Victoria seemed on the threshold of still greater population, manufacturing, and general commercial expansion. Few doubted that it would remain the central city of the Northwest. Such dreams, however, proved unrealistic. By 1901, a scant fifteen years after being designated the Canadian Pacific Railway's mainland terminus, the city of Vancouver had surpassed Victoria in

CHAPTER   III

Campbell and Simpkins Merchant Tailors was located at 88 Government Street, an example of one of the cottage industries that dotted the city. The staff was just a bit above the average size of such industries. (VCA)

Above: *The ministers and staff officials of the provincial government posed for this picture in 1898 on the steps of the legislative buildings. By the turn of the century Victoria's position in the province as the leading city had been surpassed by Vancouver, but Victoria retained political importance. (VCA)*

Facing page, top: *The International Order of the Daughters of the Empire sponsored a float in the Coronation Day parade of 1911 to celebrate the ascendancy of George V to the throne of England after the death of Edward VII. (VCA)*

Facing page, bottom: *Lumber played a large role in the city's early growth. The first mill, Parson's Bridge, was opened in Esquimalt in 1849 by the Hudson's Bay company. (VCA)*

imports, exports, manufacturing, bank clearances, head offices, and population. Vancouver had indisputably assumed the mantle of the province's major metropolis.

Vancouver's dramatic emergence has often led to the temptation to depict Victoria as a "declining" city, as if it were an also-ran in some ill-defined urban sweepstakes. This perspective does have some validity. Not only did Vancouver outdistance Victoria as a manufacturing and trading center, but in each of these central economic sectors Victoria suffered real decline. Exports and imports had fallen significantly after 1891, as had manufacturing production. While the province as a whole increased its value of production by 62 percent, Victoria's production declined by 42 percent. No Canadian city with a population in excess of 10,000 declined in manufacturing production to the extent that Victoria did. By 1901 it had dropped from fifth to twentieth place in per capita value of manufacturing output.

In other respects, however, the city continued to grow and prosper. Population continued to increase, albeit at a slower rate than in the 1880s. In fact, at the turn of the century, Victoria had moved up one notch in ranking by population—to tenth place. It would never be ranked higher. Victorians owned about one-half of all new vessel tonnage registered in British Columbia. The provincial government reaffirmed its position as capital by the costly construction of new Parliament buildings in James Bay. Tramway links to Oak Bay and a railway connection to

The British Columbia Directory of 1882-1883 included large ads for the Bank Of British Columbia and Skidegate Oil, a manufactory reliant on black sharks for its product. The harvesting of whales and sharks for oil was big business in late nineteenth-century Victoria. (PABC)

Sidney had opened up the city's immediate hinterland. Money spent on the construction of new buildings exceeded 5.5 million dollars. Significant internal improvements occurred in the areas of water, sewage, and roads.

Such development hardly sits well with the notion of decline. The issue is less a matter of winners and losers and more a matter of recognizing the type of city which Victoria was becoming and depicting the impact this transition had on those who lived there. Victoria did not decline in the 1890s; it underwent an identity crisis.

A number of factors account for the rapid expansion of the 1880s. Significantly, most of these were either linked with the seaward movement of staple products, thus representing extensions of Victoria's traditional role as an entrepot, or were associated with short-term capital-intensive construction projects. Lumber and coal continued to find ready markets in Pacific Rim countries throughout the nineteenth century. From Victoria's point of view, however, salmon and seals became even more important after 1880.

Victoria had participated in the North Pacific seal hunt as early as 1866 but it was not until market demand—a desire for full-length seal garments—increased in the 1880s that the hunt began to attract "considerable attention." While this demand fluctuated throughout the decade, a reasonable estimate of the gross revenues earned by the sealing fleet at Victoria between 1881-1891 would be three million dollars. A substantial amount of this capital remained in Victoria, spent for provisions, ammunition, chandlery, insurance, and labour. Purchase of schooners and equipment and general maintenance and refitting costs add to these routine expenditures.

The anticipation of high returns, coupled with the excitement and romance associated with sealing at that time, led to widespread community involvement. In 1891, 80 percent of the sealing fleet was locally owned and operated. Some eighty-two people owned shares in one or more of these boats. Their occupations varied from that of gentleman to lawyer, saloonkeeper, grocer, carpenter, plasterer, and labourer. For many twentieth-century Victorians the sealing fleet served the function of a mini-stock market. Those with a limited amount of capital could, along with more substantial investors like Edward Benjamin Marvin, participate in underwriting this important sector of Victoria's economy.

The fate of the seal hunt in the 1890s and early twentieth century sheds much light on the nature of Victoria's economic situation. International competition made it impossible for Victoria to control the management of this staple resource. Even in the 1880s problems between Canada and the United States over conflicting claims to

Bering Sea seal areas had led to seizures of Victoria vessels by Americans and had wreaked havoc with the sealers' profit margins. In the early 1890s the United States paid over $400,000 in compensation for these seizures and under guidelines designed to preclude overhunting, the seal trade expanded. In 1896 a record number of sixty boats left Victoria. But continued overhunting, large stockpiling, and changing fashion demand led to severe losses for the next three years. This in turn led to a reorganization of the local industry. Merchants such as Robert Patterson Rithet, Edward Marvin, and Joseph Boscowitz reluctantly began to foreclose on mortgages. Soon after the turn of the century these men and three other merchants owned over one-half of the sealing fleet. While this facilitated tighter management of wages, bulk ordering of provisions, and the ability to undercut and thus deter individual competitors, it was a case of too little, too late. Their influence did not extend beyond Victoria. Continued international competition led to sustained overkilling, depleted harvests, and a general agreement in 1911 between Great Britain, Japan, Rus-

Economic power was centralized in turn-of-the-century Victoria. This view of Rithet's Piers at the Outer Wharf provides ample evidence of the advantage accruing to Rithet through consolidation. Rithet was into the sale of dry goods and the production of iron products, and was a director of the first telephone company in the city. He also found time to be mayor. (VCA)

51

sia, and the United States to prohibit sealing in the Bering Sea.

The fate of Victoria's role in the harvesting and production of salmon sheds further light on the city's changing economic situation. Salmon canning on the Fraser River commenced in the late 1860s. From a financial and marketing point of view this increasingly important enterprise—the fastest growing export industry in the late nineteenth century—was under the thumb of Victoria's merchants. By the mid-1880s five Victoria mercantile houses successfully combined the functions of broker, financier, supplier, and insurance and marketing agent for most of the thirteen Fraser River salmon canning firms and for a good percentage of the canneries appearing on the Northern and Skeena rivers. As well as exacting a surcharge on all material required by the mainland canners, these merchants often charged more to transship goods from Victoria to New Westminster than it had cost to ship them initially from Great Britain to Victoria. At this juncture Victoria's traditional control of its mainland hinterland seemed secure.

By the early 1890s potential profits from salmon canning began to attract the interests of foreign investors. Two British-backed companies began to buy up small canneries on the Fraser. To protect their interests Victoria merchants, led by R.P. Rithet, consolidated operations into the Victoria Cannery Company. But the damage had been done. In 1892 Victoria exported 85 percent of all fish products from British Columbia. Four years later Vancouver and New Westminster equalled Victoria's output. Victoria's traditional role as an entrepot had been severely undermined. At the turn of the century investors from eastern Canada and the eastern United States effected the *coup de grâce* by merging the Victoria Canning Company with many other canneries to form the British Columbia Packing Company. These outside investors centered the company's operations at Vancouver, the most suitable site for exporting their product to foreign consumers.

It is interesting to note that Rithet appears to have been "heartily in favour" of the merger. From his perspective Victoria's entrepot role had already been undercut. By the late 1890s numerous small canneries had commenced operations, making it impossible for any existing single group to control wages, regulate catches, and standardize prices. In addition, a declining world market price for canned salmon further cut into profits. The parallel between this and the sealing industry is striking: to control costs, prevent excessive competition, and preserve accustomed profits, consolidation seemed necessary. In the case of the sealing industry, mergers stopped at the level of local Victoria operators. In the case of the salmon canning industry, an international buyer was available, and Rithet willingly entered into a larger, non-Victorian merger.

Despite its negative impact on Victoria as a whole, consolidation at least offered Rithet the possibility of continued profit in some if not all sectors of the canning industry. Or so Henry Doyle, B.C. Packer's most prominent local promoter, had promised. Doyle's belief that local entrepreneurs would control the new company "without interference from the eastern bond holders or shareholders" was, as he later realized, "violated and ignored from the very commencement." This is an important point to note. The changing structure of the province's canning industry signalled more than the curtailment of Victoria's traditional commercial and entrepreneurial dominance and Vancouver's parallel rise to power. Rather it indicated the extent of the province's economic subordination to distant, in this case, eastern Canadian investors.

This perspective provides insights into the fate of manufacturing in Victoria during the crucial last two decades of the nineteenth century. Stimulated by the construction of the Esquimalt and Nanaimo railroad and the Esquimalt Graving Dock, by expansion of the island's lumber and coal industry, and by increased shipping of all sorts in the 1880s, Victoria's manufacturing sector expanded accordingly. The Albion Iron Works, the city's largest manufacturing enterprise, employed about 260 men and occupied an entire city block by the mid-1880s. Taken over in 1882 by Robert Dunsmuir, the wealthy self-made Nanaimo coal magnate, the firm had been reorganized, and new capital was provided via the sale of shares to the omnipresent Rithet, William C. Ward, Joseph Trutch, a past lieutenant governor, and others. The iron works became a major supplier of mining equipment to Dunsmuir's collieries, of railroad equipment to the Dunsmuir-controlled E&N railway, and of marine equipment to, among others, the E&N steamship line which ran ferries between Victoria, Vancouver, Nanaimo, and Comox.

For the Albion Iron Works, and for Victoria's manufacturing sector in general, the 1890s represented a more troubled decade. Hurt by a general economic slump between 1892 and 1895, the company revived briefly during the construction of the Victoria and Sidney Railway in the late 1890s. Ultimately, however, like the salmon canners and their local merchant backers, the Albion Iron Works fell prey to eastern investors and entrepreneurs. Dramatic examples of this occurred in 1891 and again in 1898 when Dunsmuir himself ordered equipment for his mining and lumber interests from eastern manufacturers who had set up branch plants in Vancouver.

Like the canneries, the Albion Iron Works and other locally controlled iron and shipbuilding interests attempted to consolidate operations in an attempt to compete more effectively against eastern interests. For reasons which are not clear, these local operators failed to effect a successful merger in 1902. While some, like the Victoria Machinery Depot, went on to more prosperous times, others like the Albion Iron Works wound up operations before World War I.

Another important industry, opium manufacturing, also reached its business peak in these years. According to the 1891 census it ranked fifth in value of production out of fifty-four industries operating in Victoria. The island city became the center of opium production in North America in the late nineteenth century for various reasons. The United States had banned opium production and instituted prohibitive duties on the importing of the substance, making Victoria a natural site for such an industry. The city's large Chinese population was well

Conlin and Cameron Fashion Shoeing Shop was located on Pandora Avenue, just above Douglas. Many small merchant, manufactory, and service operations dotted the city. (VCA)

Above: *"Repairing of all kinds done at the shortest notice" reads the sign at the Ontario Wagon and Carriage Shop. Of interest in this photo is the presence of a young black man and a young white boy beside the four grizzled journeymen. (VCA)*

Facing page: *Proprietor Lawrence Goodacre, far right, and friends pose in front of his butcher shop in 1899. The Queen's Market, as the shop was called, had formerly been owned by Victoria's first mayor, Thomas Harris, and was noted as a favourite social rendezvous as well as Vancouver Island's first butcher shop. (VCA)*

connected with Asian suppliers and the city itself was aptly situated for the easy smuggling of goods into the United States. At its height between 1887 and 1892, the industry probably generated some 2.5 million dollars in revenue. Much of this was expended on the purchase of the semi-refined material and on duties to the Canadian government and thus did not remain in the community.

Yet in a variety of ways this industry did contribute significantly to the city's overall economy. While the eight or nine Chinese mercantile companies which controlled opium manufacturing employed only twenty to thirty workers on a full-time basis, they contracted out the production of charcoal on a part-time basis to an additional 200 to 250 Chinese in the Victoria area. In addition to paying taxes to the federal government, the manufacturers paid $500 a year to the municipality in order to obtain a licence permitting them to manufacture opium within the city limits.

This, the underside of Victoria's manufacturing, lasted until the federal government, following recommendations from a Royal Commission into the province's race relations, banned opium manufacturing in Canada in 1908.

A high number of Victoria's manufacturing establishments were small "cottage" industries employing fewer than five people in such endeavours as baking, blacksmithing, carpentry, dressmaking, shoemaking, and tailoring. In 1881 almost one-half of Victoria's manufac-

turing entities were in these areas, declining to two-fifths in 1891.

Firms of all sizes suffered real decline in the 1890s, however. Victoria's decline in number of manufacturers exceeded that of Vancouver's by 40 percent and that of the province as a whole by 16 percent. The prospects of Victoria becoming an important and diversified manufacturing center, so bright in the 1880s, had been severely dashed by the turn of the century.

Changes in Victoria's financial sector paralleled the trends in the staple and manufacturing areas. In the early 1890s one of Victoria's oldest private banks, Green Worlock & Company, collapsed. A stock market, opened in 1895 and capitalized at $250,000, closed its doors in 1898. In the 1880s the Bank of British Columbia enjoyed

record profits and its head office at Victoria headed the list in returns. By the late 1890s the bank's profits were declining and in 1900 the Toronto-based Canadian Bank of Commerce took it over, transferring its local head office to Vancouver.

A shift from seaward endeavour to continental activity underlay Victoria's and British Columbia's changing economic fortunes. This manifested itself in three ways. The nineties marked a transition between a British entrepreneurial elite well-versed in the mechanics of the old Hudson's Bay Company system to an increasingly continental-oriented and eastern-born business class. Some easterners set up operations in Victoria; most, however, favoured the mainland port of Vancouver.

Even before the completion of the Canadian Pacific

Above: *This stern-looking group of men is the legislative assembly of 1897. Increasingly, the economic impact of government proceedings became crucial to the city's economy. (VCA)*

Facing page, top: *The permanent seawall was under construction in 1903, replacing the James Bay Bridge and making possible the construction of the Empress. The old post office is the building just on the other side of the bridge while the spire in the distance is that of St. Andrew's Church. (VCA)*

Facing page, bottom: *The Driard Hotel, situated at the corner of View and Broad streets, was reputed to be one of the finest hotels "north of San Francisco." It was also renowned for the alcoholic intake of many of its patrons. (VCA)*

Railway more and more goods from eastern Canada reached Victoria via American roads. The CPR's opening in 1886 further facilitated the westward movement of goods and gradually over the next fifteen years Victoria's traditional role as an entrepot for the province was transferred to Vancouver. The railroad accelerated this trend with its Vancouver-based Empress line of steamships and its 1901 purchase of a major Victoria-based steamship operation, the Canadian Pacific Navigation Company, most of whose headquarters were then moved to Vancouver.

Perhaps the most insidious effect of this continental integration relates to the trends in manufacturing. The federal government's national policy, of which the CPR was one part, ultimately favoured eastern producers and investors. High tariffs that made it difficult to import materials and goods from the United States, coupled with low rates for the shipment of goods via the CPR from central Canada to the west, permitted large eastern-based manufacturers to take advantage of economies of scale and to compete successfully in British Columbia's

local markets.

In this context, it seems pointless to bemoan the alleged absence of dynamic entrepreneurship at the island port. Businessmen like Rithet, Ward, and others did what they could. During the 1880s the city council offered cash, tax exemptions, and free water (in various combinations) to five industries in order to attract them to the city. Three never came and the other two left as soon as the concessions expired. The city's location, at one time so crucial to its economic success, had become a liability. Seal and salmon did not develop as sustaining staples. After the late 1890s coal and lumber gradually came to supply a local and continental demand rather than a southern and foreign market and thus Victoria's role as an entrepot was further weakened. These basic changes, coupled with policy decisions made in Ottawa in which local Victorians had almost no input, led to the emergence of a different sort of Victoria from that which many had envisaged in the 1880s.

Manufacturing and wholesale trade gradually took second place to tourism and government as the mainstays of the city's economy. From its commencement, of course, Victoria had been the center of government activity. With the construction of new Parliament buildings in the 1890s, this position was reconfirmed and strengthened. This was no small success. Its mainland rivals had already attracted much business from Victoria's private

Above: *These men were lining up at the old customs house for mining permits during the Klondike Gold Rush in 1897. The Klondike was the last of the gold rushes that lined the pockets of Victoria merchants with silver, if not the elusive gold the thousands of men were seeking. Victoria served as both a transportation and provisioning center for the gold seekers. (VCA)*

Facing page: *Modest economic revival was partly tied to tourism, and the Empress Hotel was a cornerstone of that industry. This 1910 shot from the Parliament buildings captures the hotel before its expansion and before the construction of the Belmont and other blocks around it. (VCA)*

sector. Vancouver and New Westminster also coveted the position of capital. In early 1890 the mainland and island had almost equal representation in the Legislative Assembly. Victoria's representatives more often than not enjoyed the power of the premier's post and of many important "cabinet" positions. The Parliament buildings, built at a cost of $923,000, were begun under the administration of Theodore Davie, a Victoria lawyer, and finished under the administration of John H. Turner, a Victoria businessman and past Victoria mayor. It was none too soon. Electoral redistribution in 1898 and again in 1902 irrevocably shifted the political balance of power from the island and Victoria to the mainland and its growing urban centers.

The Parliament buildings ensured the government's continued economic presence. They also acted as prime attractions for the second and fast-emerging prop of the city's economy: tourism. As early as the 1870s Victoria was included as a point of interest in continental tours organized by a New York and Boston travel

firm. Throughout the later part of the century cruisers from San Francisco to Alaska stopped at Victoria where "tourists land, scatter themselves through the city, and leave in a few hours. . . ." During the 1880s the city became more than simply a casual stopping point. John Jessop, the Dominion's local immigration agent, estimated that over 13,000 tourists visited Victoria in 1884. Two years later a close observer noted that "Victoria is a favorite winter resort not only for the people of B.C. but for many living south of the line, while in the summer it is crowded by tourists whose numbers annually increase." In the same period the city began to advertise its attractions to world travellers as not simply a "summer resort" but also a haven for "health seekers." The year following the completion of the new Parliament buildings, some 70,000 tourists visited the city. By the turn of the century a Tourist Development Association was established and in 1901 the local board of trade published its first tourist booklet.

Perhaps the most fitting symbol of the demise of manufacturing and the rise of the tourist era occurred in December 1901 when the board of trade wrote to the Canadian Pacific Railway suggesting that it construct a first class tourist hotel in the city. As Mayor Alexander Gilmore McCandless admitted, "the establishment of such a hotel in our midst would make us a CPR town. At present we are practically off the map." Two years later the city sweetened the offer with a "bonus" of free land and a fifteen-year exemption from tax and water charges. Unlike the city's failures to attract industry via

"bonusing," the result in the tourist sector must be labelled an outstanding success. The Empress Hotel, open for business in 1908, quickly became one of the city's most famous landmarks. The Canadian Pacific Railway, which many Victorians blamed for the abrupt decline of the city's traditional economy, proved instrumental in developing an alternative.

The emergence of this revised *raison d'etre* provided the broad context for substantial change in Victoria during the last decade of the nineteenth century. Probably because everybody used it, water received the greatest attention from Victoria's city leaders. Yet even in this area significant improvement in water quality awaited a real or impending crisis. Fears of a diptheria epidemic due to foul water provided to the city by the privately owned Spring Ridge Waterworks Company led to the construction of a city-owned system in the 1870s. After the expenditure of $200,000, however, there seemed to be little improvement. A local doctor testified that "he didn't drink any more [water] than was necessary—in fact he preferred not to drink it at all." Small wonder that in 1891 Victoria produced about one-half of all the mineral water manufactured in British Columbia.

Pressure for an upgrading of the system grew as population density increased in the 1880s. Residents of the "high districts"—members of the affluent class such as William Ward and family—complained that in the summer the water pressure was so low that their residences were dry. A series of costly fires in 1886 prompted the city to lay a larger main between it and Beaver Lake in

Above: *By the early twentieth century the city was modernizing rapidly. The Goldstream pumping station was a costly endeavour to assure a water supply in keeping with a modernizing city. (VCA)*

Facing page, top: *The city hall received a facelift in 1891 when towers were added to the original structure. These workmen seem more intent on posing for the camera than finishing the job. (PABC)*

Facing page, bottom: *In 1906 the Victoria City Library moved out of city hall and into this new structure, partly financed by Andrew Carnegie. The funding was controversial because the American philanthropist was linked to the Homestead riots and anti-monarchy groups. (VCA)*

1888. Yet the following year the fire department complained that water from city hydrants "is not sufficient to reach the roof of a three-storey building."

A smallpox epidemic in the early 1890s—which some felt was in part facilitated by the "impurity" of the water supply—coupled with the constant fear of an uncontrollable fire led to a substantial upgrading of Victoria's water system. Land surrounding the watershed area of Beaver Lake, from which the city drew its water, was purchased to prevent cows and other barnyard animals from polluting it. A new filtering and main system was installed—the old system being a "veritable repository of filth." In 1908 a sixteen-million-gallon reservoir at Smith's Hill completed the ambitious revamping.

Since the gold rush, sewage disposal had been a contentious issue. Grand jury reports in the 1860s lamented the lack of civic concern and the evident danger to general health. A ravine paralleling Johnson Street and cutting through the heart of town had by 1890 acted for the past thirty years as a mainly open and often stagnant central sewer collecting the wastes of the many businesses and residences along it. Reporting on general conditions in Victoria in May 1885, the American consul had this to say:

If this town were not situated as it is on the extreme point of the island fanned by the cleansing breezes from the Straits of Fuca and the winds invigorated by passing over the continually snow-capped surrounding moun-

tains, I think it might prove a very hot bed for the cholera because of the filthy condition of most of the streets and rear yards of the central buildings. It is dirtier than Cologne. There is no sewerage whatsoever and the water closets are primitive, much as they were years ago in Washington and the sanitary police force is small and inefficient. . . .

In 1880, after investigating systems in operation in major eastern Canadian cities, Victoria committed an initial $300,000 for the construction of the city's first comprehensive sewage plan. By 1900 some 75 percent of the residents were served by the resulting sanitary system. Interestingly, and perhaps typifying Victoria's changing image, the industrial reserve across the harbour and opposite the city's central business district remained the only significant area not served by sewers.

Following the fires of 1886, a new building code provided for the construction of only brick or stone buildings in the downtown core and made it impossible

Above: *Late nineteenth-century Victoria was dotted with saloons. The Garrick's Head was one of the most infamous, as this shot may suggest. (VCA)*

Facing page: *While the legal restrictions on Indians were never as overtly racist, the island's first residents suffered many of the same ills as the Chinese. Here, four coast Indians pose for the camera. Contact with whites almost eliminated many bands on the coast. (VCA)*

to alter existing and rapidly deteriorating wood structures. Enforced by a building inspector, this code resulted in a substantial upgrading of the city's core throughout the 1890s. For example, in 1893 and 1894 some fifty wooden buildings were demolished in the "central portion of the city." These measures also helped keep the city reasonably free of major fires in the period.

By the 1890s Victorians had come to believe that their city's economic health was directly dependent on the quality of the environment.

Victoria's medical health officer put it most succinctly in his 1893 annual report:

I have on several occasions dwelt on the necessity of proper attention being paid to the drainage and sewerage of the city. We cannot in the interest of the public health or of commerce, afford to remain at a standstill. Ours is a tourists' city. Its beautiful location and surroundings draw yearly a large number of this class of people among us. It is on the highroad to the Orient, Australia, and Alaska and these different lines bring us large numbers of the best class of tourists—people of

wealth. We should then endeavor to make our city as beautiful and healthful as possible.

Matters of political economy had merged with the needs of the general populace to produce a sustained upgrading of Victoria's living conditions. Without this merger the significant activity of the 1890s would not have occurred. Yet this is not the whole story. There was a prior and more deeply ingrained motive which underlay reform in these areas.

During the 1880s thousands of Chinese were brought to British Columbia by white contractors to build the Canadian Pacific and later the Esquimalt and Nanaimo railways. Even before the completion of the railroads many of these Chinese located in Victoria. A census taken by the municipality in May 1886 indicated that almost one in three of the city's residents were Chinese. They were not welcome. The attitude of a white owner of a small grocery store typified Victoria's view:

They are immoral, dirty, corrupt, and are not fit to take the place of domestic servants as they are a curse to the young. They use every endeavour to seduce our females of all ages. Knowing their evil habits are kept a secret. They are a stumbling block to all advancements as they take and fill positions as by right belongs to white men and women who would develop the country and increase population of a sound Anglo-Saxon race—people who would open up the country and fight for it too. They are increasing. . . . Chinamen send all their spare cash to

China. Whitemen and women spend all right here. . . . Him no sabby fight. We must fight for his home and our own.

The city's white business elite and its white working-class population were at one in their desire to rid the marketplace of Chinese competition. Due in part to the federal government's use of disallowance, provincial legislation seemed unable to stem the inflow. The local courts would not permit the city to use its powers in licensing to exact heavy fees from businesses, like wash houses and laundries, owned and operated by Chinese. Municipal powers in the areas of health and sanitation thus offered an alternative strategy. As the virulently anti-Chinese local labour paper *The Industrial News* explained, strict laws in these areas would be more effective than suspect provincial legislation "in ridding us" of the Chinese.

This was not an entirely novel idea. One of the first sanitation by-laws passed by the city, it will be recalled, had been designed to keep the Indian women out of Victoria. It is therefore not surprising that the 1880s and 1890s saw a number of stringent by-laws passed ostensibly to improve Victoria's general living conditions—but in reality to effect the speedy removal of the Chinese from the city. A cubic air by-law requiring 384 cubic feet of space for each resident in a room proved to be moderately effective. In December 1885, 175 Chinese were arrested, but as only thirty could pay the fine and the local jail was too small to incarcerate the remainder, punishment was spotty.

The Chinese had few alternatives. Victoria's role as an entrepot for the shipment of supplies to mainland Chinese declined abruptly upon completion of the CPR and the return to Asia of many Chinese railroad workers. Several of the largest Chinese wholesale houses went bankrupt in the 1880s. Increasingly poverty-ridden, few could afford to live outside the crowded boundaries of Chinatown—the 1886 census reported that 1,435 Chinese lived on Cormorant Street alone. Not surprisingly, police charge books indicate numerous repeat violations of the cubic air by-law and of other "sanitation" measures relating to faulty water closets, uncovered cesspools, and garbage removal.

The smallpox epidemic of 1892—apparently brought to Victoria by a Chinese visitor—forced Victoria's British elite to cease relying solely on punitive measures aimed mainly at one section of the city and to implement structural change. Not that punishment was eliminated. During late 1892 and early 1893, in the aftermath of the epidemic, over 100 Chinese were prosecuted under the cubic air by-law. Yet, probably frightened by the possibility of a recurrence of smallpox—in the past only Indians and Chinese had contracted the disease, this time whites died too—the city broadened its target area. In 1894 the sanitary inspector and two policemen "made a systematic and thorough inspection of all the premises in the city." Sanitary violations extended well beyond Chinatown: 2,500 notices were issued to clear up various nuisances and 1,000 cesspits were "ordered to be cleaned up and filled up."

In addition to broadening the implementation of the sanitary regulations, the city council looked to structural reform as a final protection against the recurrence of a major epidemic. After laying 34,000 feet of sewage pipe, the city, urged by its health officer, installed sewers in Chinatown in 1894. Given that sanitary measures up to this point had been used to "rid" the city of the Chinese, the installation of sewers—a permanent structure—symbolized the *de facto* acceptance of the Chinese presence by Victoria's white elite.

Infrastructural development also took place in areas not as directly related to health and sanitation. In almost all cases, however, such development was closely tied to the city's emerging economic base. The fact that by 1889 Victoria allegedly had more telephone users per capita than any other North American city figured prominently in the city's promotional literature. More substantial evidence of the city's receptiveness to technological change occurred in the area of lighting. Victoria was one of the first cities in Canada to own and operate an electric lighting system.

Long dissatisfied with the "high rates and unsatisfactory service" of the Victoria Gas Company (founded in 1860), the council finally authorized two local businessmen—Gilbert McMicking and Edgar Crow Baker—to install a state-of-the-art electrical system in 1883. Within a year these men were asking council to take over the operation of the business, their own capital proving insufficient to the task. Reluctantly council agreed and after one unsuccessful attempt persuaded the ratepayers in September 1885 to authorize the borrowing of $16,000 to pay for and upgrade the system. By 1897 the plant worked well enough to allow the city to outline its downtown buildings with 3,000 lightbulbs, initially to celebrate Queen Victoria's Diamond Jubilee, and ultimately to attract tourists.

Tourists could reach Victoria via the CPR's extensive ferry system and by American ferry companies. Once there, after 1886 they could travel to Nanaimo by rail in two and one-half hours with the option of disembarking at any of seven stops along the way. After the late 1890s they could also travel to Sidney via the Victoria and Sidney Railway. Within the city itself, the most common mode of transportation prior to the 1890s was the horse-driven hack, the precursor of the modern taxicab.

In the mid-1860s members of Victoria's elite complained that the five or six hacks in the city did not permit full attendance at plays and operas. By the mid-1880s the nature of the complaint had changed. Now hacks controlled the streets. As one bemused resident put it, "no city in the world of double size has half the hacks of Victoria." With seeming impunity twenty-eight of the forty-two hack drivers who plied Victoria's streets in 1886 ignored city council's demands for licence payments. They did agree to stop halting two abreast and blocking traffic on Government Street where they lined up for fares—as often as not leaving their hacks unattended while they patiently waited in the nearest bar. Perhaps this is why the city council's "Hack Commit-

Top: *Government Street in 1892 was Victoria's busiest and most important roadway. Just visible at the top of the street is a streetcar. Streetcar service had begun just two years earlier and had not yet reached the length of Government Street. Streetcars ran in Victoria for fifty-eight years, until 1948. (VCA)*

Bottom: *Street railways relieved much of the transportation confusion engendered by the hacks. This view is from about 1895, looking north down Douglas Street from Yates. The city hall clock is on the left while the spire in the distance is that of St. John's Anglican Church, "The Iron Church," on the site of present-day Hudson's Bay Company. (VCA)*

tee" warned the police "to caution hackdrivers who are in the habit of waiting hire and leaving the line and throwing up in the gutters."

By the mid-1880s hack driving was becoming a big business. One-fifth of the hacks were owned by one company and four individuals owned two or more. The reality of this mode of transportation is not adequately captured by the horse-driven carriage in which tourists ride today in downtown Victoria. "The cab-stand on Government Street is highly objectionable," the medical health officer warned in 1894, not only because it detracted from Victoria as a tourist spot "but there is a much more important—the sanitary—reason why it should be done away with in the most frequented street of the city." As one old-time Victorian reminisced, "Horses being there all day, it would get a lot of manure around, of course, and when it was dry like that and there was a wind blowing all kinds of dust that deep, everything was flying up and down."

A partial solution to this problem was the establishment of a street railway system that commenced operation in 1890 as a privately owned enterprise. Soon after the turn of the century the reorganized company ran routes that served most of the city's populated areas and which opened up—often to inside speculators—much of Victoria's choicest suburban areas.

In fact Victoria's residential area grew immensely during the last decades of the nineteenth century. By the early 1890s residential areas extended past Rock Bay and beyond Bay Street in the north, to Cook Street in the east, and dramatically filled out James Bay to the south. Multi-acre estates began to be developed in Rock-land—like Craigdarroch Castle built by the Dunsmuirs—and in the Gorge Road area. These very neatly and fortuitously added to the attractions offered tourists.

Changes also took place within the city's commercial core. Those major industries that persisted in the area gradually shifted from Victoria's inner harbour to Esquimalt. Wholesale functions continued to cluster on Wharf Street but for the first time retail and general commercial outlets began to separate and move up Government and Douglas streets where, along with a growing number of office buildings and churches, they extended into the center of the city.

Cultural affairs continued to attract elite support and participation. Most concerts—performed by local amateur societies as well as by professional international touring groups—and most theatrical presentations were well attended. Press reviews of the many amateur presentations were often revealingly prefaced by disclaimers such as "judged as a performance by amateurs" or "There were those who thought that the amateurs had undertaken too heavy a task . . . and at times . . . it looked as though they were right. . . ," but on the whole such reviews were supportive and encouraging and gave the impression that cultural affairs in Victoria were in a healthy state. Via Sunday outdoor concerts at Beacon Hill Park, the head of the Gorge, and in Oak Bay, attempts were made to attract "the masses, our retail men, their employees, and a greater portion of the working class," as one correspondent put it, for whom "Sunday is the only available day" to enjoy "the privilege of two hours' enjoyment and elevation." Most such recitals were reportedly well attended.

As historians of other western Canadian urban centres have demonstrated, the late nineteenth and early twentieth century was an era of dramatic increase in sports participation. City councils willingly provided land space and other facilities seeing in such activity the means of inculcating "manly" virtues—discipline, strength, loyalty, and morality—in the younger generation. Similar development occurred in Victoria. Sports events became increasingly varied. Baseball, football, cricket, and horse racing vied for space at Beacon Hill, the city's major park. Shooting, lacrosse, and rowing attracted strong followings. The James Bay and other athletic associations were formed. In the eyes of the president of the local cricket club, it was essential to encourage "to the utmost among the rising generation the practice of games, which, perfectly harmless in themselves in every way, conduce to health and bodily vigour and which are the means of affording an outlet for the energies of youth which might, otherwise, be found in injurious and undesirable direction."

This varied development and change affected different classes in the city in different ways. The city's police reports, when looked at in isolation, seem to indicate a stable if not declining crime rate throughout the period. In the mid-1880s fourteen constables patrolled the city of some 11,000 people and their main problem seemed to be a high incidence of chicken thievery. Four plainclothesmen successfully apprehended the "chicken-ring," run by unemployed and starving Chinese. Just under one-half of all arrests in 1884 concerned vagrancy and drunk and disorderly conduct.

Yet when the local statistics for police arrests are compared with those for other Canadian towns and cities

Above: This 1890 group photo of Victoria's finest illustrates the strong British connection. The uniform, up until the 1940s, was the same as that worn by London bobbies. Throughout the nineteenth century the commissioner was British-born and most of the police possessed a British and/or military background.

Facing page: The James Bay Athletic Association, seen here in the foreground of this view from the Parliament buildings circa 1897, was home of Victoria's earliest sporting organization. (VCA)

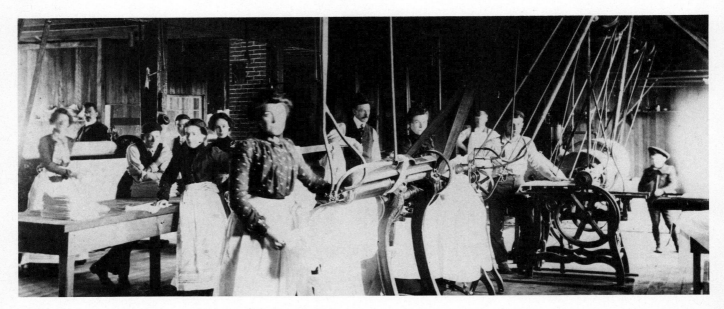

a potentially different light is cast on the incidence of crime in Victoria. The island city boasted the second highest ratio of arrests per 1,000 people of thirty Canadian urban centers in the early 1890s. No constabulary arrested more drunks per 1,000 people than did Victoria's finest. A Royal Commission on the Liquor Trade reported in 1895 that this was a very high ratio, but offered no explanation other than to comment on Victoria's "large floating population" (they intended no pun), the implication being that the local residents were not the main delinquents.

In 1889, at any rate, the police committee happily reported that "the morals of the city are improving," even though prostitution was certainly thriving. A police report in 1886 listed twenty "houses of ill fame" in Victoria and counted 138 prostitutes not including "Indian women . . . who have no fix'd place of abode as they are coming and leaving the city all the time."

Industrial labourers suffered the most from the economic changes in this period. During the 1880s they enjoyed high wages but were also subject to a relatively high cost of living. During the 1890s, when manufacturing declined, their job security ended and many left the area. In fact, during the nineties there is evidence of a deterioration of labour-management relations in Victoria. By 1892 there were at least ten different unions in the city. These included the American Brotherhood of Carpenters, the International Typographical Union, the International Moulders and Foundry Workers, and smaller unions for painters, tailors, plasterers, musicians, cigar makers, and seamen. When the Dunsmuirs took over Victoria's largest industrial concern, the Albion Iron Works, in the early 1880s, they brought with them

their confrontational attitude toward workers. As a result Albion Iron Works soon refused to hire union workers and during the 1890s "serious labour problems" beset the factory. The lack of worker success in this sector probably influenced the Victoria local of the Carpenters Union to advise their members against strike activity at the turn of the century. Victoria's business elite adopted a strong anti-union stand with virtual impunity. The changing economic emphasis in the 1890s increasingly relegated the industrial worker to the sideline.

The Chinese were, of course, already on the sidelines. While about one in three of Victoria's residents were Chinese in 1886, their proportion of the population had dropped to one in seven by 1901, although the total number of Chinese remained roughly constant. Their prospects, however, seemed little altered. This can be indicated in two rather symbolic ways.

One of the more distinguished and successful architects of the era, Francis Rattenbury, designed many of the Victoria elite's stately houses. His allocation of space is revealing. The drawing room, living room, and bedrooms were open, large, and airy. Located at the rear of the house, the kitchen, by contrast, was cramped and dark. A small staircase off the kitchen led to an even smaller room on the door to which Rattenbury often inscribed on his plans "Chinaman."

On a larger scale, the message is the same. Victoria promoted itself to tourists as a "bit of Old England." The Tourist Development Association's first pamphlet stressed how British the city was and how like Old England the pastoral hinterland seemed. Just as in the houses that the elite built, there was little room for the non-Anglo-Saxon in the emerging economy that the

same elite managed.

If the industrial worker and the Chinese had few options available to them in response to changes in the economy, the same was not true of Victoria's business elite. Certainly the wealthy Dunsmuirs did not suffer from the closure of the Albion Iron Works. Similarly the Rithets, Wards, Bakers, Turners, and Marvins continued to build and live in opulent houses; entertain and be entertained in lavish splendour; found and join prestigious private clubs, like the Union Club; sit on the city council and Legislative Assembly; and, in short, control the city's destiny in a political, social, and economic sense. Between 1880 and 1900 the nature of Victoria's fortunes changed dramatically, but the composition of its ruling class and the attitudes which that class promoted changed imperceptibly if at all.

Above: *The Salvation Army founded a Victoria chapter in 1897 and has a distinguished history in the city. This shot captured the army band on a picnic in Oak Bay just before 1900. (VCA)*

Facing page: *There were many labouring jobs for women in the late eighteenth century, relative to the total positions available. Many small manufactories as well as laundries employed female workers. This picture suggests a gender balance at Victoria Steam Laundry. (VCA)*

The Legacy of a Boom

For Victoria, the new century started slowly. The Klondike gold rush of the late 1890s had not re-created the frenzied speculation of forty years earlier. In Victoria, as long-time merchant Jacob Hunter Todd complained, "making money appears to be a thing of the past." The abrupt closure of the Imperial Naval Base at Esquimalt in 1905—after four decades of continuous activity—seemed to confirm Todd's prophecy. Great Britain left and with her went 1,000 men who spent $700,000 annually in the area. The 120 engineers and gunners sent out as replacements by the Canadian government hardly filled the gap. Spurned by the Mother Country and by Ottawa, Victoria became, in the eyes of one contemporary observer, "the most conservative and perhaps sluggish city in the Canadian Northwest."

Given this context, it is little wonder that the boom which engulfed the city between 1907 and 1913 "astonished old timers and indeed the province at large." Activity within the island port rivalled that of any period in its past. Civic expenditures and civic borrowing skyrocketed. Private building broke all records. Land values escalated. Mayor Alfred J. Morley assured an all too sympathetic audience that:

Victoria of 1910, replete with unprecedented growth, progress, and prosperity, its citizens imbued with a steadfast spirit of broad and generous enterprise, stands as a tangible guarantee of the greater Victoria of the immediate future.

The boom did indeed set the context for the future; but it was a future very different from that envisaged by the mayor and his audience in 1910.

From one perspective it would have been remarkable had Victoria not undergone dramatic development in the pre-World War I era. The city "boomed" amidst a general atmosphere of unbridled optimism and intense growth in western Canada. British Columbia's population increased by 220 percent. Some of this tide of humanity washed ashore at the island port. Victoria gained

CHAPTER IV

Victoria Transfer Company's Tally Ho carriage rounds Shoal Bay at the turn of the century. The Tally Ho wagons that ply city streets today date back to the previous century. (VCA)

Above: *The early twentieth-century city retained much of the grace of an earlier time. Here the Elworthy and Boggs families enjoy a picnic in 1902. Notice the Chinese servant in the top right corner, a not unusual occurrence in a household of standing. (VCA)*

Facing page, top: *Professor Wickens posed for this 1908 photo with his Children's Orchestra at their sixteenth annual concert. Traditional high culture was kept alive for the children of certain families through endeavours such as these, and for adults through the city's extensive artistic community. (VCA)*

Facing page, bottom: *The first decade of the century saw the introduction and multiplication of the automobile in the city. The first auto is reputed to have been that of a Dr. E.C. Hart who first travelled the streets in 1903. There seems to be a certain excitement in standing still in an auto as late as 1910 if this photo is any indication. (VCA)*

a respectable 52 percent, more than doubling its growth rate of the previous decade.

To a degree the characteristics of this population influx helped set the stage for the ensuing boom. Throughout this period the American consul marvelled at the wealth many brought with them. Attracted by the relatively pleasant climate, many came to retire. As the consul explained to a prospective dealer in motorboats, "Victoria possesses a large leisure class and has received during the last two years [1906 and 1907] a large number of wealthy former citizens of Manitoba and Ontario." As a result the city was ripe for the sale, not only of motorboats, but also of automobiles—the consul, in fact, felt that in proportion to population no North American city had more of the latter. A survey of the Dominion and Postal Savings Bank and of the seven private banks operating in the city in October 1908 revealed that they had 2.5 million dollars in their respective "savings departments." It remained to be seen just how and where this influx of idle capital would be invested.

The not-so-wealthy also arrived. According to one resident, if the well-to-do British tended to build estates and hide behind six-foot walls, other arrivals gave the

E.G. Prior and Company showed off the "Stickney Junior Gasoline Engine" at the Willows Exhibition Grounds in 1905. Like many local businessmen, Prior was also involved in politics and served a very short term as provincial premier in 1902-1903 and as lieutenant-governor in 1919-1920. (VCA)

city a strong "cosmopolitan" flavour:

Go down to the wharves, almost any day and a perfect babel of tongues greet you. In the space of a block you may hear Chinook, Chinese, Japanese, Hindu, Korean, Russian, French, Norwegian, as well as the master English language.

While many of these people stayed only a short time, enough persisted to provide a ready source of labour in the pre-World War I era.

Rapid escalation of American investment in Vancouver Island's timber resources complemented the arrival of wealthy residents and provided some employment for prospective labourers. Led by lumbermen from the eastern and midwestern United States, American investors "poured their money" into British Columbia, believing that the province's timber represented the last on the continent that could be obtained at low rates.

Anticipated change in the commercial sphere also helped set the foundation for dramatic growth. The pending completion of the Panama Canal (opened in 1914) would, Victorians believed, resuscitate shipping and commerce at the island port. The Grand Trunk Pacific instituted a line of steamers connecting Victoria, Prince Rupert, Vancouver, and Seattle. The city committed some funds for dock and harbour improvements and successfully petitioned provincial and federal agencies for more. When the federal government in 1911 granted three million dollars to construct a large shipping dock at Esquimalt with a completion date timed to coincide with the opening of the Panama Canal, the area's commercial future seemed assured.

While fuel for a boom existed, the resulting fire appeared curiously artificial. Certainly a great deal of money—more than at any time in the city's past—changed hands. Bank clearings during 1907 were the largest ever and transactions during 1912 more than tripled that record. But what did this unprecedented movement of money represent?

American investment in island resources did lead to further transportational development in Victoria's hinterland. In 1909, for example, the Esquimalt and Nanaimo Railway announced that it would spend over $300,000 upgrading its facilities. This investment, however, did not lead to significant industrial growth within the city itself. Almost all of the record amount of construction in 1907 consisted of office buildings, hotels, and residences. No factories or large manufactories were established. This held true throughout the boom period. The industrial sector received only 14 percent of the $23,223,327 spent on building between 1907 and the end of 1913.

Top: *Produce was farmed within the city limits well into the 1920s. Here a potato farm, located south of the city and north of Beacon Hill Park, is cultivated around 1920. This farm is part of the Invertavish Nursery Gardens, located between present-day Rupert, Heywood, and Southgate streets. (VCA)*

Above: *The machine age came most dramatically with the introduction of automobiles to the city. This is the interior of the Victoria Motor Company's machine shop circa 1912, one of many small businesses spawned by the popularity of the automobile. (VCA)*

Small manufactories continued to provide much of the city's employment circa 1905. This is the Jeune Brothers Sail Loft on Johnson Street. (VCA)

In 1911 gross value of manufacturing production still fell short of the amount attained in 1891 and per capita value of production had not reached the 1881 figure. Over the past decade, the three other major British Columbian cities—Vancouver, New Westminster, and Nanaimo—had increased their numbers of manufactories; Victoria's declined by one-third. Quite clearly Victoria's money did not underwrite industrial growth.

Some of this capital flowed into the commercial sphere. Federal money certainly upgraded both Victoria's and Esquimalt's harbour facilities in this period. Exports, however, rarely exceeded the 1901 figure. Although imports and customs duties did increase, the former barely reached one-quarter that of Vancouver. Traditionally the port which received the highest registration of new shipping in the province, Victoria attained only one-half the tonnage registered at Vancouver be-

Top: *The sign on the truck reads "Victoria Corporation Blacksmith Shop," a good example of the services the city needed in 1913. The driver in this picture is identified as J. Cruickshank and the mechanic foreman as Bill Yule. (VCA)*

Above: *The Brentwood Bay generating station was constructed in 1912 to supplement Victoria's main supply of electric power from Jordan River. The Brentwood station also supplied power for the electric railway which ran from the city up the peninsula to Deep Cove. (VCA)*

One of the city's leading citizens, Thomas Shotbolt, built this mansion near Fairfield and Foul Bay roads in the mid-1880s. Shotbolt was one of the promoters of street lighting and railway systems and arranged for a streetcar turnabout outside his driveway. (VCA)

tween 1910 and 1914.

The major part of the boom consisted of two inter-related parts: private spending on home construction and real estate transactions, and a combination of private and public spending on infrastructural improvement. Activity in one depended on development in the other. The building of houses and the opening of subdivisions necessitated extension of services, waterworks, roads, and sidewalks. Promises of virtually unlimited manufacturing and commercial growth facilitated dramatic expansion and expenditure in the housing and infrastructural sectors. It is noteworthy that those "boosters" who were loudest in their assurances of a buoyant economic future invested little in industry and trade and much in real estate and housing.

There were approximately 3,100 residences in Victoria at the beginning of 1907. By the end of 1913 there were over 7,600. These included homes for the wealthy but also, and significantly, mass-produced subdivision housing, which increased during the peak boom years of 1911-1913. Although the number of individual local contractors had more than doubled from forty-six in 1905, major construction companies began to dominate the scene. Similarly, although the number of real estate agents proliferated several large ones are reputed to have controlled much of the market.

The annually elected city councils did their best to augment this rapid expansion. This included the granting of "the largest paving contract ever awarded by a Canadian city" covering eighty-nine streets at a cost of $1,150,000. During the same period sixty miles of concrete sidewalks were laid. During 1909 the city employed an average of 900 workers per day at an annual cost of over $600,000 in wages. In 1911 the work force increased to 1,137 per day and the payroll increased to over one million dollars for the year. In addition to these operations, the city continued the ambitious and costly revamping of its water system by linking the municipality to Sooke Lake. In an attempt to beautify the city, the council also embarked on a pioneering program of boulevard development.

As a result of these and other expenditures, the city's debenture debt had reached 18.9 million dollars by 1917 and represented a per capita burden 1.7 times greater than that of Vancouver. Almost all of this had been contracted before the outbreak of World War I and all but 5.4 million dollars had been borrowed after 1910.

Apart from its size, Victoria's debt possessed at least one further distinguishing characteristic. Local improvement bonds comprised 45 percent of its total debenture outlay. By comparison Vancouver's local improvement issues only reached 28 percent of its total bonded indebtedness. At a general level this point is significant for two reasons. Local improvement bonds required the approval of those city residents whose property abutted the areas being upgraded. They also required that the same residents pay a certain proportion of the debt for the various improvements undertaken. In Victoria's case some 75 percent of local improvement borrowings was the sole responsibility of the property owners involved. The city at large expected to pay only 25 percent of these costs, an extremely low percentage compared to the practice in eastern Canadian cities at that time.

This leads to the second and perhaps most revealing point about the nature of Victoria's boom. A provincial act required the repayment of these loans in ten equal annual installments. As a result some Victorians were expected to pay a very high price for the pleasure of living in the Garden City. Just who were they? After a thorough investigation into the state of Victoria's finances—paid for by concerned city residents in 1922— Dr. Adam Shortt, an economist for the University of Toronto, concluded:

In some of the most heavily burdened portions of the city, so anxious were the speculative subdividers to get their attractively improved property on the market, that they were quite willing to saddle their prospective customers with the whole cost of the local improvements, the amount of which was not revealed to the new owners until some considerable time after the lots had passed into their possession. The civic authorities, on their part, some of them being considerably interested in the sale of the newly improved properties, had little hesitation in incurring very heavy obligations, the repayment of which, it was claimed, would not fall upon the city, which was acting merely as an agent of the property owners in expending the money and collecting from individual owners their assigned proportions.

In other words this system of financing local improvements was a speculator's dream. Land developers would "vote" for upgrading in the expectation that they would have sold the affected property before any improvement costs became due. Since no bond could be issued before the completion and final cost accounting of the upgrading had occurred, the odds were strongly in the favour of the experienced speculator/land developer. The fact that over 50 percent of the city council members for whom occupations could be found were, in 1911 and 1912, contractors or realtors, makes it easier to understand the council's positive attitude toward local improvements. And finally since the older "settled" Victorians, most of whom already lived in "improved" areas, believed that

Above: *Saunders established his grocery store just after the gold rush of 1858 and built it into one of Victoria's leading retail outlets. The liquor department is shown here about 1910 with Peter Bugslag behind the counter. (VCA)*

Facing page: *These grim-faced men are members of the city engineering department in the 1920s in their office on the third floor of city hall. (VCA)*

they would never have to pay much for the development of other people's property, there was no wider entrenched interest willing to oppose the system.

In yet another way the nature of municipal financing during the boom period facilitated the activities of the knowledgeable speculator/land developer. During the period of greatest speculation—from 1909 to the middle of 1912—assessed value of land was well below the land's actual market price. When the land boom began to collapse, the assessed value belatedly began to increase, peaking in 1914. By that time most experienced speculators had already unloaded their land onto prospective homeowners and unsuccessful speculators. Those who profited most were therefore taxed least.

The money expended by the city during the boom years was raised by the sale of municipal debentures in England. In this Victoria was not alone. In fact almost all cities and provinces and the federal government were busy doing the same thing. By mid-1912 the British bond market had become saturated with Canadian securities. Yet at that very moment Victoria's financial situation had reached a crisis. Its account at the Bank of British North America was three million dollars overdrawn—due to the interim financing of unfinished local improvements—and its agents for the sale of bonds in London informed Mayor Beckwith that "it would be ab-

solutely impossible to dispose of any City of Victoria bonds [in London] except at a sacrifice price. . . . " One informed local financier reported that "Beck[with] and council at wits' end over financial position. . . . Their account is being peddled at two if not more banks. . . . Situation is disastrous." In this case the city's financial agent, the Toronto-based Dominion Securities Company, sold enough bonds in the American market to stave off the "disaster." During the following three decades, the city lurched from one crisis to the next in a series of attempts to deal with the financial consequences of the spending policies of the boom years.

They looked to the provincial government for relief. The province, alarmed at the financial situation in Victoria and in several other municipalities, reorganized the Municipal Act in 1914. The general result was the loss of some autonomy for Victoria in exchange for the province reviewing all municipal bond issues, thus giving to these debentures greater credibility in foreign markets. The loss of autonomy was a price the city council accepted, albeit reluctantly.

On its own initiative the city engaged in what can only charitably be described as creative accounting designed both to disguise illegal financial manoeuvres and to obscure the desperate nature of the city's finances from the eyes of local citizens and distant investors. For

example, the full value of an ever increasing sum of tax arrears was listed as an unqualified asset in the city's annual statements. Not only was the practice continued when there was almost no possibility of full collection, but the tax arrears were also used as collateral for interim bank financing which at times approached one million dollars. Although this was manipulation of a customary sort—almost all British Columbian municipalities did it—and did not break any laws, it did serve to hide Victoria's real debt situation from the view of the average city resident.

The systematic bleeding of funds set up under legislation to retire outstanding local improvement debentures was a matter of a different sort. Money required by law for these funds was instead used to retire bank loans and to meet current expenses. "In the case of a private individual," a local lawyer asserted, such behaviour "would be classed as embezzlement." The answer offered by those responsible reflected the gravity of the situation. "So much money only was collected and we did the best we could with it." They believed no other course was possible to prevent bankruptcy.

To meet the local improvement bond payments coming due throughout 1922-1924, ten years after they were issued and for which no funds were on hand for repayment, the city applied to the provincial assembly for legislation which would allow them to float a $3-million refunding issue. The assembly granted the right but in so doing both the city and the province ignored the fact that such debentures required ratification by city rate-payers. Ratification was never sought.

The manoeuvres employed by the city in this period were so various and complicated that the provincial inspector of municipalities admitted to the attorney general in 1923 that it was hard to know what was what.

The consolidation of Victoria's debt in the mid-1920s —meaning the city at large assumed responsibility for all local improvement debts—coupled with what seemed to be the beginnings of a modest economic revival, gave the municipality a short breathing space before the depression era of the 1930s.

The stratagems employed by the city to protect its financial standing in British and American bondmarkets took place against a backdrop of increasing human misery. Although overshadowed by the First World War, the nature of the boom and its ultimate collapse had a profound impact on the lives of those living in the Garden City.

As early as February 1909 astute local observers realized that the city, in providing jobs to the many labourers who were arriving in the area, "tended greatly to relieve the labour problem." The escalation of city activity helped create what turned out to be a vicious circle: the more the city expended on various projects, the more the city attracted prospective employees. The more the city boasted of its prosperity, of the impending growth of commerce and industry, and of the area's climatic splendour, the greater the number of working-class families who uprooted and moved west.

By November 1911 the city had hired some 2,000 men and private construction employed a similar number. Despite this, the local paper and informed observers agreed that "there never have been as many idle and un-employed men in Victoria as at the present time." The local office of the British Columbia Federation of Labour wrote to a London, England, newspaper to warn prospective immigrants that now "is not a favourable time" for going to the island port. A "congested" labour market, high rents, high cost of living, and inadequate wages awaited the foolhardy. The Victoria *Daily Times* advised that no jobs in commerce or general manufacturing existed in the city.

The same paper also admitted that "among organized labor there has been considerable dissatisfaction with the terms of employment." And so there was. During 1912 and 1913 there were at least seven strikes involving about 800 workers totalling some 15,270 man-days lost. Most of these strikes were broken by the importation of

new labour. As the local Plumbers' Union representative admitted in January 1913 after a bitter twenty-eight-day strike against fifteen firms, the supply of men was greater than the number of jobs, so they called the strike off. By April 1913 the situation had worsened. Plumbers' representative George Litster lamented, "We are making earnest endeavours to organize the city as it was before," but due to employer recruiting in the United States and Canada, the union had "many idle members" and prospects looked dim.

More than surplus workers militated against successful labour activity. In April 1912 the Canadian Mineral Rubber Company, the paving enterprise which had won the city's large contract, paid its labourers $2.45 an hour, five cents lower than the wage labourers received in Victoria in 1908. Given the escalation in cost of living during that time it is not surprising that 350 labourers struck for higher wages. The company ignored their demands, hired new workers from the surplus in the city, and continued operations without interruption.

A major reason for the company's successful defiance of such a large number of dissatisfied workers is suggested by the observations of one local resident, penned during the paving strike of April 1912:

Construction work in Victoria still goes merrily on notwithstanding strikes and petty hindrances by street lawyers and loquacious idlers, who are allowed to talk without material hindrance, but who run against the iron hand of provincial police when work is interfered with.

At times Victoria's police did more than simply keep guard. With the sanction of the Board of Police Commissioners, which overruled protests from the Victoria Trades and Labour Congress, local prisoners had been used as strikebreakers. The chain gang was alive and well in the early twentieth century. Despite the justice of

Top: *One of the city's largest employers continued to be R.P. Rithet. With a fortune made in sealing and shipping in the nineteenth century, Rithet expanded into various pursuits. His staff posed for this picture in front of his Wharf Street establishment. (VCA)*

Bottom: *During the 1916 British Columbia Electric Company strike this car provided rides at ten cents per passenger. (VCA)*

Top: *Two of Victoria's regiments were the Fiftieth Gordon High-landers and the Eighty-eighth Victoria Fusiliers. This is a photo of the Eighty-eighth Battalion of which both these units formed a part. (VCA)*

Above: *The SS* Algerine *was used to train local naval cadets in the art of seamanship. This is a 1918 shot from the inner harbour with the Empress Hotel clearly visible in the background. (VCA)*

the employee's cause, local authority in Victoria protected the employer.

Bereft of funds and heavily in debt, the city began to lay off workers in January 1913. "You can see them on the streets everywhere you go," the American consul wrote in May. "The trouble is there is nothing for them to do." By November, 2,000 lacked jobs. The city attempted to operate on staggered three-day shifts to provide part-time work for a larger number of people. By November 1914, however, the city could only afford to pay one dollar a day and few could support families on three dollars a week.

War, of course, ultimately provided the city some eco-

The First World War pulled many women out of their homes and into the work force. These women worked the orchards of Victoria during the harvests of the war years. (VCA)

Victoria-Esquimalt area and local merchants prospered. Yet unemployment persisted. In December 1914, 1,300 unemployed men remained registered at the city's Central Employment Bureau—an agency that Victoria, like many other Canadian municipalities, had set up to help workers find jobs. Six months later, the number of registrants had increased to 2,200 and the cost of food had increased by 20 percent. The city, forced to cut back operations in order to convince eastern and foreign bondholders that they were capable of running a tight economic ship, could not hire or provide direct relief to the unemployed.

It was not until 1916 that the war effort began to foster a significant number of jobs for Victoria's unemployed. The federal government announced that it would grant massive subsidies to stimulate a shipbuilding industry on the coast. For a brief period of time Victoria led the province in responding to the subsidy offer. Although many of the skilled shipworkers were sent out from the east—in June 1917 some 500 to 600 mechanics and ship's carpenters arrived to work for the newly formed Foundation Company, Ltd.—general employment for locals increased throughout 1916 and 1917 in almost all sectors but that of the building and construction trades.

With war's end, so too ended the economic renaissance. Veterans returned. Competition for a shrinking number of jobs intensified. From May 1917 to mid-1919, the city experienced its most volatile period in labour relations. Spearheaded by the machinists, a series of strikes hit the shipyards and general iron metal industries. The workers argued for increased wages and union recognition. A strike by 2,000 machinists and shipbuilders in May 1918 received little sympathy from city businessmen. As the local representative of the federal *Labour Gazette* reported, "the loss of wages will have a bad effect on business—Victoria never having had such a large payroll."

Unrest in the city peaked in June 1919 when a massive rally was held in Royal Athletic Park to show support for the city of Winnipeg's famous General Strike. In late June, as a further indication of support, the metal

nomic relief. In addition to drawing away surplus labour —British Columbia had the highest per capita volunteer ratio in Canada—new economic opportunities did emerge. Although deep-sea steamship business fell off by at least 20 percent, Esquimalt once again bristled with military-related activity. By late 1915 some 2,000 to 3,000 enlisted personnel were concentrated in the

trades closed down thirteen firms when 5,372 men walked out.

During the immediate postwar period, labour in Victoria achieved some successes. Machinists, shipyard workers, teachers, firemen, garbagemen, electrical workers, mariners, lighthouse tenders, and cereal workers all struck successfully for higher wages. These gains were, however, short-lived. Pay scales at the major machine shops were sliced by fifty cents in January 1921, and in July 1924 the principal milling companies cut their salaries by 10 percent. Layoffs accompanied the salary cuts.

The city, still burdened by severe financial constraints, attempted to attract more permanent industry. In 1921 it established an Industrial Committee, which after a year's operation admitted that "as much has not been accomplished as could have been wished for." Attempts in the 1920s to attract a motion picture industry, an airport, a grain elevator, a cold storage plant, and a woollen mill had mixed results at best. The simple fact of the matter was that the city was in no financial position to be able to offer attractive subsidies. That, coupled with a geographical position relatively isolated from major markets, made the task of establishing a manufacturing sector other than shipbuilding difficult indeed.

There can be little doubt that the principal promoters of Victoria's ill-fated boom realized this. Although they imported workers to develop the city and construct houses, those houses were for other people. A November 1915 survey of residential housing in Victoria reported that there had been little done to provide housing facilities for working classes. Rather the city attracted other classes: well-to-do retirees, government employees, and retailers who supplied local and tourist needs. While those most intimately involved in profiting from the boom talked of wholesale trade and manufacturing, in actuality they provided an in-

frastructure suitable for people who worked in other sectors.

In fact, for Victoria's oldest established elite encounters with the working class were uncomfortable at best. Senator William John MacDonald, one of the city's first residents and a highly successful land speculator, complained in 1912 of packed tramcars:

On the platform you are very often crowded with workingmen smoking their pipes. I have not anything to say against the workingmen. At the same time you don't want to run against men covered with dirt and cement. It is improper and the conductors know it is improper and they should disallow it.

Throughout the 1920s there was an "exodus" of working-class people from Victoria. As the American consul reported in December 1923, however, the situation differed among the "better classes." Only a few of "these people" had left the city "and a much larger number" had taken their place. During the 1920s Victoria's age distribution began to reflect an increased number of retirees. By the end of the decade almost 9 percent of the municipality's residents were over sixty-five. No Canadian city had a higher percentage of this age group, and none have exceeded Victoria in this category since that time.

These population changes are further corroborated by the trends in school enrolment. Up to the early war years the superintendent for Victoria schools complained annually of "congestion," limited space, and a shortage of teachers. "Intolerable" conditions prevailed at the turn of the century. By 1911 student-teacher ratios of sixty to one were not uncommon. Superintendent Edward B. Paul criticized the city council, which had to

Above: *The city's public education system expanded in the first two decades of the century when over a dozen schools were constructed. This is a photo of the Vic West School and one of its classes about 1918. (VCA)*

Facing page: *Some complained about the class of people who frequented the tramcars, and it is rumoured that this open observation car was used as a drinking car on more than one occasion. (VCA)*

raise roughly three-quarters of the municipality's funding of education, for delaying the passage of a by-law providing funds for new construction. In 1914 student enrolment in elementary schools exceeded 5,000, dropping slightly during the war years and peaking in 1919 at 5,800. Enrolment dropped almost every year during the 1920s, however, and by 1930 it had dipped to 4,772.

It therefore seems clear that Victoria underwent a significant demographic change and a significant class change during the 1920s. Its overall population, however, remained virtually stable. The census of 1931 reported an advance of less than 300 people (0.9 percent). Since local births would probably more than account for this growth, the 1920s was an era of net outward migration. The 39,082 people living in the city in 1931 were considerably fewer than the number who had lived and worked there during the boom years of 1911 and 1912.

One further characteristic of that boom helps to explain why the twenties did not "roar" in Victoria. Most of the revenue raised by the city to repay the massive debts incurred during the "boom" period came from one source—a single tax on land, a levy which excluded the value of any improvements. This policy, instituted by referendum in 1911 near the height of the boom, had a profound impact on Victoria's subsequent development. Victoria was not alone in relying on the single tax. Vancouver had implemented a similar policy in 1910. Victoria, however, persisted in this strategy longer than most western cities. As a result a significant number of its citizens suffered unduly.

As the boom collapsed, the market value of land rapidly declined. The city then faced the following dilemma: should the rate of taxation be increased or should the assessment (as opposed to market) value be kept at an inflated level? The city decided in favour of the latter course with the result that by 1920 the market value was only 25 percent of the assessed value of land in Victoria. Despite moratoriums (especially for soldiers) and other extended payback schemes, increasing numbers of Victorians were unable to meet the taxes exacted on such artificially inflated land values. By 1921 the city, due to unpaid taxes, had reclaimed land which amounted to almost 10 percent of the municipality's total assessment valuation.

These statistics point to several underlying realities. Obviously increasing numbers of citizens were forced to sacrifice their property at annual tax sales. Undoubtedly many of these lots had been purchased in the boom period when expectations had seemed so bright. As Adam Shortt commented, by "far the most numerous class" negatively affected by the boom and single tax were:

those who held land previous to the boom periods, or have bought with the object of establishing homes for themselves with the accompaniment of a garden, toward which most laudable purpose the climate and situation of Victoria are so favorable.

Perhaps even more revealing of the extent of tight money, if not dramatic poverty (although the latter cer-

What is now Camosun College was formerly home to both Victoria College, the precursor of the University of Victoria, and the Normal School, which was established in 1915 to staff the schools of the province with qualified instructors. (VCA)

tainly existed), was the fact that so few of the properties offered at the annual tax sales actually found purchasers. And of course the more lots reverted to the city, the smaller the base from which the municipality could draw income under the single tax system. This problem was further compounded by the increased tendency of those who worked in Victoria to live outside the city in the newly developed suburbs of Oak Bay, the Uplands, and Saanich.

This combination of factors created a very modern problem for Victoria in the 1920s: how to maintain a viable downtown core area. In the words of a local lawyer who specialized in municipal law:

Our efficient transportation systems, the advent of the cheap automobile, the salubrity of our climate, which enable the pleasant use of motors all the year round, makes it easy and advisable for an increasingly large number of people to live in outside semi-rural places, doing all their business in the large centres. The circumscribed areas of business of the large centres are

This view of Marsden News Shop on the southwest corner of Yates and Government streets is dated circa 1900. The man in the top hat is Tommy Burnes, the owner of several leading hotels in Victoria. (VCA)

congested in the daylight, and these and many blocks around are deserted at night. Such almost exclusively residential municipalities as Oak Bay . . . are built up. Taxation is naturally lower there because they do not supply the services the business municipality does. . . .

Side by side with the manicured lawns of the Empress and the Parliament buildings, with the stately residences of James Bay and the Rockland neighbourhoods, with lush city parks and golf courses, stood, in the words of a 1928 planning memorandum, a "maze of lanes with shacks, and dilapidated houses and vacant lots filled with rubbish and weeds." Ever optimistic, the city council in 1927 and again in 1929 implemented zoning plans that reflected the heady optimism of the 1910-1912 boom period. As a result excessive waterfront and other land was reserved for industrial usage—yet sufficient industry never appeared and land better suited to commercial and residential development remained undeveloped. The boom's legacy ran deep.

One of the few positive economic spin-offs from the boom years was the enhancement of facilities for tourists. The Empress Hotel acquired a major structural addition and other hotels were refurbished and/or newly constructed. This concern for providing attractions for tourists extended into the 1920s when the city, via a referendum in 1924, granted the Canadian Pacific Railway

Company, owners of the Empress, free water, a land site, and easement to construct an amusement/convention center known as the Crystal Gardens.

Indeed, throughout this period the city remained alert to the economic benefits of an increased tourist trade. In 1916 the council took steps to enforce "orderly conduct" on the owners of "sight-seeing vehicles" and hack drivers who, during the summer tourist season, commonly hassled arrivals at the Belleville Street Dock with "shouting, with or without megaphones, undesirable solicitations, noisy and other unsuitable conduct." An investigating committee concluded that such behaviour, which belied the city's sedate, conservative image, "is detrimental to the City of Victoria . . . and . . . should be abolished."

In 1923 the city council granted $25,000 to the Victoria and Island Development Association to promote tourism in the Victoria region. In conjunction with the neighbouring municipality of Saanich, the city opened the area's first auto camp to better provide for this increasing sector of the tourist trade. Throughout the 1920s car ferries were introduced and expanded, linking the island directly with Washington State, with Vancouver, and with up-island areas via the Mill Bay ferry.

If the support system for tourists and their mode of travel had changed since the early twentieth century, Victoria's image as disseminated by the local Publicity Bureau and Tourist Development Association remained constant. All who would listen were assured that the Garden City continued to be a replica of "Old England." It little mattered that as early as 1901, 46 percent of Victoria's population had been born in Canada and that by 1931, 51 percent were Canadian-born. Nor did it matter that one of the pre-eminent propagandists for the "bit of old England" slogan, the American-born George Warren, manager of the Publicity Bureau, had never once been to Great Britain. In fact, during the 1920s the proportion of British-born in the city began a decline which has not yet ended. In 1921 they represented 38 percent of the population, and in 1931 they were about one-third.

Nor did it seem to matter to the predominantly American tourists that there was much that was American about this highly touted British spot. While many of the city's prominent architects—like A. Maxwell Muir, Thomas Sorby, and Francis Rattenbury—were British-born and influenced by Victorian styles, some, like Muir, had come to Victoria via California, and all were receptive to American design. Much of the speculative construction during the boom years aped the standard California bungalow. Even the newly constructed Union Club of 1912—built for the upper crust of Victoria's British male society—had been designed by Loring P. Rexford, an architect from San Francisco.

American influence was no less prominent in certain branches of the media. While some of the older residents apparently felt that American-manufactured films exhibited "too much indecent exposure," it nonetheless remained true that in the 1920s 80 percent of all films shown in the city were produced south of the border. In the opinion of the American consul, taste and demand for pictures in Victoria "are practically the same as the average American city." A similar demand dominated the taste of the reading public. According to a survey of monthly sales of periodicals at a local Victoria newsstand in 1929, 67.6 percent of the purchases were of American publications, 18.5 percent of British periodicals, and only 13.9 percent were of Canadian magazines. Even "the most important annual event" in the city, the Victoria Day celebration, has been dominated by American bands up to the present day.

This mix of British image, American influence, and

Canadian presence worked. Tourists, mainly American, came and liked what they saw. As Robert H.B. Ker, president of Victoria's Publicity Bureau, asserted in 1927, Victoria was "no longer a side trip but a main objective." And that was what really mattered. After all, what other economic alternative was there?

One of many large questions affecting the city during the boom period concerned the settlement of the Songhees Reserve. This tract of land comprised 112 acres situated on Victoria's inner harbour. Since at least 1858 Victoria's white leaders had attempted, by purchase or other means, to acquire the land and evacuate the Indians from such close proximity to the town's centre. Nor were Victoria's motives simply economic. As we have seen, the white citizens of Victoria had taken great pains to seal its borders against native infiltration. They finally succeeded when the province took formal possession of the reserve in April 1911 at a total cost of $755,000, of which $433,619 went directly to the Indians. The rest went to the Hudson's Bay Company (or more precisely the affiliated Puget Sound Agricultural Company) for new land (170 acres in Esquimalt) for the Songhees and to provincial negotiators for a job well done. Now the city could expand its port, attract new industry, and build new railroads, integrated terminals, and connecting bridges. Of course, the boom soon burst and the super port, railway yards, and industry never developed to the degree anticipated.

By white men's values, the Songhees Indians fared relatively well. They acquired a new reserve, larger than the old one and in many respects better situated. They also acquired more money than they had ever had. In the process, however, their traditional values were irrevocably undermined, to which a dollar value is very difficult to assign. The boom's legacy, in this respect, was fraught with ambiguity—for all parties involved.

The boom years also affected the lives of Victoria's Chinese population. In the years before 1907 a head tax to the extent of $500 had been levied on all Chinese entering Canada. In Victoria white labour organizations and petty merchants continued to demand an absolute closure to all Asiatic immigration. Despite these attitudes most contemporary sources suggest that during the boom period Chinese were more welcomed in the city than at any time in the recent past—perhaps than at any time since the gold rush of the early 1860s. The reason was economic. Servants were in short supply and other, often menial construction jobs, were, for a short period, filled by Chinese.

Despite these, albeit fleeting, opportunities, few new Chinese took up residence in Victoria. The attitude of the Chinese already residing in the city might have

Agricultural labour was one of the few jobs open to Chinese immigrants. A group of Chinese berry pickers pose in the early twentieth century. (VCA)

been at least partly responsible for this relatively small increase. In 1899, 1904, and 1913 the local Chinese Consolidated Benevolent Association sent back to China evocatively worded arguments designed to discourage further immigration into British Columbia. They argued that jobs did not exist, discrimination was widespread, and claimed that "a sea of sorrow" awaited those who "listen to the [immigration] agents from Hong Kong." While these remarks were meant to apply to an area much wider than Victoria, it is possible that since the association located their headquarters in that city, its local members were able to convince new arrivals to try their luck elsewhere.

Even though they attempted to control their numbers, the Chinese people in Victoria continued to be treated as a separate and second-class group. In British Columbia extremely liberal provisions governed the right to vote in municipal elections. In 1911 if a male or female, over

These are, presumably, the proprietors of the Japanese Bazaar located at 45 Government Street. Though most Asians began as labourers, by the 1920s many were moving into retail concerns, some even setting up shop in "white" parts of cities. Such economic success led to further pressure on government to limit immigration. (VCA)

twenty-one years of age and a British subject, owned or occupied municipal land assessed at $100 or over, he or she had the right to vote. Much to some local politicians' chagrin, Victoria even gave hotel dwellers and delinquent taxpayers the franchise. The same right, however, did not extend to Chinese, Japanese, or Hindus. Since becoming a lawyer, pharmacist, or chartered accountant in British Columbia depended on being on a voters' list, the Chinese suffered greatly by the exclusion.

Between 1903 and 1920 Victoria's medical health officer consistently reported on the city's low death rate, often referring to it as the lowest for any Canadian city. In 1913, for example, he referred to the mortality rate of 6.67 per 1,000 as "a record of which the citizens have cause to be proud." He did not mention the death rate of the city's Chinese population—it stood at 17.6 per thousand. This figure was surpassed in 1918, when the Chinese death rate reached twenty-three per thousand. The mortality figures for the city as a whole never came close to these rates.

Just as the general living conditions of Victoria's Chinese remained oppressive, so too did the attitude of the white majority. As late as 1932, Victoria's elite-dominated Island Arts and Crafts Club—founded in 1909, it was Victoria's principal art group until after World War II—refused to accept Lee Nam, a respected Chinese painter, as a member.

Throughout the 1920s the city attempted to restrict the right of Asians to engage in various business pursuits. Instead of simply denying them the right—as the city had attempted to do and failed when it did not receive legal sanction earlier—longtime city council member W.J. Sargent suggested in 1924 that those businesses which hired more Chinese than British-born subjects should pay, on a sliding scale, a higher license fee. While this proposal received much support within the city council, it did not receive the necessary provincial backing.

In 1929 the council requested its solicitor to write to other municipalities for advice on how to circumscribe Chinese activity. When no helpful information was received, the council then decided to write to Cape Town, South Africa, for "complete information" concerning their policies "re regulation of business and residential locations of negroes and Orientals." Cape Town sent back a copy of a local Royal Commission into the Oriental problem along with other "encouraging" advice. While no restrictive measures emerged, this attempt to solicit ideas from a place such as South Africa illustrates the depth of anti-Chinese feeling in the city at that time.

This desire to segregate rather than integrate Victo-

ria's Chinese and white communities surfaced in the practice of that most "integrative" of institutions, the city's school system. In 1922 all Chinese students were sent to the North Ward to attend, according to the local Chinese Benevolent Association, "deserted school buildings which they [the trustees] have cast aside and which are overgrown with weeds." Their parents, disgusted with the continual rebuffing of their attempts to attain the rights that Victoria's white population so freely enjoyed, withdrew their children from the school system for the remainder of the year. Only after much discussion did the school board, in 1924, permit Chinese students with adequate knowledge of English to attend integrated classes.

Obviously the boom years did not eradicate deep-set racial antagonisms. The boom left a very limited positive legacy. Only the tourist sector benefitted. The overall legacy which the greed, blundering, and rampant speculations of those years bequeathed is best described in terms of human deprivation, stunted growth, and financial chaos. As the city struggled to redress and recover from its past, a Depression struck, the likes of which North America had never experienced. In Victoria's case the Depression years represented a continuance, albeit at more intense levels, of several themes evident during most of the post-boom years.

By 1932 conditions in Victoria were grave indeed. Tourism dropped dramatically. Shipbuilding and repairs had ground to a standstill. Local lumber mills closed operation to await better times. The military establishment at Esquimalt had shrunk to just above the 1906 level. During the first six months of 1930, eight bankruptcies occurred, totalling over $210,000 in liabilities. From April 1929 to April 1931 there was a 50 percent decline in retail business.

Direct relief expenditures by the city in 1932 reached $374,621. The provincial and federal governments contributed $319,102. According to one source over 12 percent of the city's citizens received direct aid from the municipality in that year. Not surprisingly Victoria, having enjoyed only two or three years of precarious financial solvency since 1912, soon crumbled under the burden. Sinking funds were raided in 1934 and again in 1935. Bonds had to be refunded and property reversions mounted. Tax yields declined and license revenues dwindled. The city's infrastructure, to which almost nothing had been done since 1914, demanded "immediate attention." With provincial sanction, the mayor contacted Toronto and London bondholders and after protracted negotiations announced a further refunding and consolidation of Victoria's mounting debt. Once again the city had to take dramatic financial action in order to main-

Above: *The Chinese community attempted to educate themselves through the construction of their own school close to Chinatown, on Fisgard Street. This is the grand opening in 1909 of the second school, one that is still standing today. (VCA)*

Right: *The first auto camps in the city opened in the 1920s to take advantage of this growing market. After declining in the early years of the 1930s, tourism reached record levels by the last years of the decade and has remained a staple of the city's economy since. This auto camp was located at 99 Gorge Road. (VCA)*

tain at least the image of financial stability.

At the social level, the Depression took a severe toll. Between 1930 and 1933 crimes against property rose by 1,000 percent over the previous three-year period. Vagrancy arrests skyrocketed as single, unemployed males moved from up-island to Victoria seeking refuge and employment. The elderly, who depended on interest income from stock and debentures, suffered severely from the 1929 crash and only slowly recovered in the late 1930s.

With the rest of Canada, Victoria gradually rebounded following 1936. World demand for lumber picked up. Tourism, by the late 1930s, attained record levels. Stocks and bonds moved slowly upward and, as a result of that and of tourism, retail business moved ahead. The city, as it had on the eve of the Depression, was slowly regaining solidity on the eve of World War II.

But there is more to the history of Victoria during the Depression years than that of economic decline and slow recovery. Three other developments, all visible before the 1930s, accelerated during that decade. Because of their long-term importance, these issues deserve brief consideration.

Victoria's relations with the neighbouring centers of Saanich, Oak Bay, and Esquimalt deteriorated. The city saw itself as the "milch cow" suckled by the adjoining municipalities and receiving little in return. Its solution was to absorb the outlying areas into one body—the City of Victoria. The smaller municipalities would have none of it. They believed that Victorians desired amalgamation only in order to shift their onerous debt onto other people's shoulders and they refused to accept any responsibility for the existence of that debt. Relations deteriorated throughout the thirties, with court cases necessary to settle a number of specific grievances. Amalgamation, buttressed by commissioned reports from "experts," resurfaced many times since that decade, but the results remained the same.

A second trend noticeable during the 1920s, the greying of Victoria, continued at a rapid pace throughout the 1930s. Coupled with the Depression, this trend had an obvious impact on the process of family formation in the Greater Victoria region. Marriages fell abruptly in mid-decade; so too did births. In fact for four of those years the death rate surpassed the birth rate. When this first happened in 1935, the local medical health officer felt that Greater Victoria was "unique" in showing a "negative Vital Index." This "misfortune," he acknowledged in 1938, meant that "the average age of our population must be rapidly increasing." And so it was. Although the rate of marriage and birth began to increase in the early forties, it remains true that by the end of the Depression Victoria deserved recognition as Canada's foremost retirement center.

Alongside the needs of tourists and retirees, the servicing of government increasingly set the agenda for the city's economic future. The Depression also had an impact in this traditional sector. Throughout North America it had become evident that governments would have to undertake larger roles than they had in the past. From Victoria's point of view, larger governments meant more dollars in the local economy. By the end of the decade local employment at all three levels of government had mushroomed and exceeded employment in any other single category in the city.

In retrospect, then, the 1930s witnessed the acceleration of significant trends already visible in the earlier post-boom era. By 1940 Victoria had come of age in more ways than one.

Modern Victoria: Leader or Laggard?

Victoria's location is one of its most distinctive characteristics. Its role as a port, its small manufacturing centre, and its attractiveness to tourists and retirees can all be explained by its island site and pleasant climate. Furthermore, its reputation for a relaxed, slow-paced style of living is compatible with a commonplace image of island life. In 1894 a visitor noted that "Victorians are proverbial for an easy distribution of time between office and home." Seventy-five years later the city's director of community development informed an American correspondent that that description "succinctly labels us—we hope for all time." In this view the Island City became a safe harbour sheltered from the hectic, competitive pace of the modern world.

For many, this is a beguiling image. It has, however, led to a tendency by commentators to contrast Victoria with other, usually mainland, municipalities. The city's distinctiveness is stressed; its commonality is ignored. A closer look suggests that not only has Victoria been buffeted by many of the problems and challenges facing

North American urban centers today, but that with reference to several major trends in modern society, the Island City stands at the cutting edge of change.

The troubles which Victoria confronted during the inter-war years, for example, affected to a greater or lesser degree all western Canadian cities. The fruits of excessive boosterism combined with a sluggish regional and national economy during most of the twenties and the Depression of the thirties to preclude expansion, necessitate retrenchment, accentuate social hardship, and undermine local municipal autonomy. Increasingly, western Canadian cities lost independent creative power as regional, provincial, and federal governments assumed an ever larger role in areas of social welfare, economic policy, and revenue collection. In Victoria's case this led to reliance on higher governments for funding powers, transfer payments, and following the banning of industrial bonusing in the early 1930s, the initiation of certain economic programmes.

The war years intensified municipal dependence on

CHAPTER *V*

The Crystal Gardens boasted both North America's largest indoor swimming pool and Victoria's newest dining and dancing facilities. This 1950 shot catches patrons relaxing under the palms while others use the pool below. Today the Crystal Gardens houses shops and a reception hall while the pool area has been converted to a botanical garden. (VCA)

Above: *Tourists relax near a floral welcome to Victoria along the inner harbour. Photo by Barbara Gundle*

Right: *Colorful street vendors peddle a variety of wares. Photo by Bob Garlick*

Facing page, top: *Victoria Golf Course skirts the Strait of Juan de Fuca and provides a majestic backdrop for a round of golf. Photo by Bob Garlick*

Facing page, bottom: *The annual Harbour Festival draws thousands to the inner harbour for music, exhibitions, and a street dance. Photo by Bob Garlick*

When launched in 1947 the Chinook *was tagged the "Queen Elizabeth of the inland seas." Built for $2.5 million, the* Chinook *plied the waters between Victoria and Seattle and was noted for its comfort and elegance. (VCA)*

powers and events outside of city boundaries. Naturally enough, the war effort took top priority. Victoria's citizens, as they had in World War I, contributed with gusto. Those who stayed formed Air Raid Precaution units, "ready," as Mayor Andrew McGavin asserted in 1943, "to deal with every emergency." Following the bombing of Pearl Harbor, Victoria saw itself as being "in the front line" and along with Vancouver, the city spearheaded the drive to round up and remove all Japanese, whether Canadian citizens or not, from coastal areas. A siege mentality enveloped the region.

Far from being a haven, the city bristled with activity. By 1941, 3,490 enlisted personnel were stationed in the area. As in World War I, general economic activity, especially in the retail and industrial sectors, spurted ahead. This imposed demand severely strained the city's limited industrial capacity. "In Victoria," one of the two major shipbuilders admitted, "there is no reservoir of labour, particularly in the skilled trades." Labour, as in the previous war, had to be imported from the east.

Working conditions were far from ideal. Although production was impressive, the federal government's imposition of continuous seven-day shifts upset traditional workplace rhythm and undermined morale. As A. Clyde, the business agent of the local Boilermakers and Iron Shipbuilder's Union, testified before a Royal Commission on shipyards in August 1942:

I have been at this business since 1894. They have been in the habit of getting Saturday afternoon or night off and (I don't do it myself) many of them like a glass of beer and after they drink beer on Saturday night, they don't feel like working on Sunday. Sunday is a day of rest. . . . Now it will take a dictator before you break them into a seven-day plan. . . . I know the men I am talking about; I have lived amongst them all my life. They work up to Saturday night—and then on Sunday? Jesus Christ they will not work for on Sunday!

The municipality faced the problem of housing this sudden influx of labourers and Armed Service personnel and their families. Due to fiscal restraints and depression little new accommodation had been built in the two decades before the war. Federal restrictions on the use of construction and lumber materials made it difficult for Victoria's private sector to respond to the acute housing shortage. Single family dwellings took in boarders.

Some familiar landmarks are visible in this early 1950s view of Douglas Street. At the end of Douglas is the Hudson's Bay Company, the city hall spire is next to it, and on the left, in front of Woolworth's, is the Francis Jeweler's clock. (VCA)

According to the health officer, in 1942 "practically every available space that is roofed over is being used." The number of cases involving communicable diseases was almost five and a half times greater than in 1939 owing to "the fact that homes originally occupied by one family are now sheltering four or more families with no possible facilities of isolation."

The federal government responded to the nationwide problem—at the beginning of World War II Canada was approximately 250,000 houses short of need—by creating a housing agency called Wartime Housing, Ltd. For a variety of reasons, it had only limited success in Victoria. Residents in James Bay, the site of the Victoria Machinery Depot, resisted the construction of what they feared would be shacks and slums. By October 1943 labour turnover at the depot reached 300 per month. Workers stayed only long enough to acquire a skill before moving to centres with more adequate housing for themselves and their families.

With the return of veterans, the housing shortage persisted throughout the late 1940s. By January 1948, 1,500 families were waiting for housing and, according to a local newspaper, Victoria in 1946 was one of the most "congested" municipalities in North America, averaging 5.7 people per unit. Conflict between the federal housing agency and local builders continued after the war as both competed for scarce construction materials. Widespread strike activity in the timber and construction sectors intensified an already unstable social situation. Decreased production by wartime industries, however, led to large layoffs and to an exodus of labourers from

the Victoria region. The housing pressure gradually eased—property values began to drop in August 1949—and congestion abated. The island city paused to regroup and confront the postwar era.

Among the many priorities, one overshadowed all the others. As newly appointed city manager Cecil Wyatt put it, the city's financial position continued to be in a "lamentable" state. It possessed the highest per capita debt burden of the sixteen largest Canadian cities. Since no financial institution would bid for a large issue of bonds in 1951, Wyatt had to make "a special trip to the east" and even then only sold them "at a large financial loss to the city."

Before undertaking needed infrastructural development—almost no work had been done on roads, sewers, or waterworks since the pre-World War I era—the city had to break out of its "financial strait-jacket." Wyatt implemented reform on two fronts. A "pay-as-you-go policy" helped reestablish financial respectability in the eyes of eastern bond houses. The municipality could then undertake needed road and sewage repairs with the local ratepayers assuming 75 percent of the repayment costs. In contrast to the pre-World War I experience, the city

VICTORIA

Above: *Each year thousands of sailors and sailboats descend on Victoria for the Swiftsure Classic, a demanding two-day race covering 136 miles of Pacific swells. Photo by Bob Garlick*

Facing page, top: *Victoria marks Canada Day in its annual celebration on the lawns of the legislative buildings. Photo by Bob Garlick*

Facing page, bottom: *The Empress Hotel serves as a backdrop for Harbour Festival celebrations. Photo by Bob Garlick*

carefully monitored the cost of these improvements and the general economy permitted a satisfactory repayment programme. Wyatt also revamped policies governing the sale of reverted lands. A legacy of the boom years and the Depression, these holdings were "abnormally high in comparison with other Canadian municipalities" and they were not being sold at current market rates. Throughout the 1950s the city sold these properties at the highest rates possible, using the proceeds (over 1.6 million dollars by 1960) to underwrite its pay-as-you-go policy. By these means, the city kept its taxation rate—compared to that of other municipalities—at a reasonable level.

In 1951 Wyatt pointed out that current debt payments were in part facilitated by money received from the sale of assets to the Greater Victoria Water District. These annual payments, which exceeded one quarter of a million dollars, would end in 1963 and the city had no plans other than an onerous increase in the tax rate to meet the resulting shortfall. As a result Wyatt set up a fund via the sale of the city-owned grain elevator and via a special tax to meet the increased debt charges of the sixties.

Wyatt also initiated a series of internal reforms. City council committees were reduced, accounting procedures centralized, and coordination between the various city departments placed in the city manager's hands. Before this time, as Mayor Percy Beale Scurrah remarked in 1957, each department had been "a little empire unto itself." Under those conditions, Wyatt explained, it was virtually impossible to exert "any control over expenditures." With the introduction of the city manager structure a much needed degree of continuity and of professionalism began to characterize the exercise of city affairs.

There were other priorities. Some members of the chamber of commerce argued that the city must take a more active role in attracting industry, without which, they believed, no city could expand and prosper in the new era. The situation was so grim that even tiny Moose Jaw had had success in attracting industry from Victoria to its prairie site.

The explanation for this is not hard to find. During the war years, as D.K. Kennedy, Victoria's building inspector, noted, residential and commercial construction significantly overshadowed industrial building in the city. The reverse occurred in eastern Canada. While eastern Canada was taking steps to convert war industries into postwar manufactories, British Columbia would find itself with only the industries established before the war.

Vancouver and the east would receive the business after the war. The shadow as well as the reality of eastern hegemony blocked significant industrial development in Victoria. The trend to eastern industrial domination, already evident at the turn of the century, intensified during and after World War II.

Victoria was thus the victim of a national industrial policy. At a more local level, Victoria suffered a further competitive disadvantage following the war. In 1907 the city had successfully lobbied for freight parity with Vancouver in rates to British Columbia and prairie points. This agreement, Victoria's industrialists argued, made it possible for the city to maintain at least a reasonable level of industrial activity. In 1949 the railways ended the arrangement and raised Victoria's costs by a differential of some 100 miles. Protests to the Board of Transport Commissioners succeeded in forcing a partial revocation in certain classifications, but on the average rates remained higher and the city's industrial potential suffered.

Nor did the increased efficiency of ferry service between Victoria and Vancouver—a direct link to Sidney from Tsawwassen was established in July 1960—lead to industrial gain for the island. Although the local shipbuilding sector did profit temporarily from ferry construction, in the long run Victoria's industrial sector suffered.

Service industries—those businesses founded to supply a local region—from that point had to compete directly with larger firms in Vancouver. Factors of scale coupled with lower transport costs made it possible for the larger Vancouver firms to ship their product and sell at competitive prices in the lower island region. As a result both the service industries—the bulk of Victoria's manufacturing sector—and the local wholesale trade sustained losses and many closed their doors for good.

Workers in the industrial sector consistently declined in postwar Victoria. Viewed from a larger perspective, this is not surprising. Victoria was far from unique in this regard. The same trend held true for British Columbia and for Canada. In terms of the percent of workers' participation, Canada, and indeed North America as a whole, was becoming deindustrialized. And like other major western Canadian cities, Victoria was below national employment percentage levels in manufacturing. Only the degree of decline set Victoria apart. By 1971 fewer workers, expressed as a percentage of the total labour force, worked in Victoria than in any other major western Canadian city. In Victoria the rate of participation was already low and the decline was more dramatic.

But the point remains: the pace of deindustrialization in Victoria put the city in the forefront of a major social and economic trend in North American urban life. Like it or not, the city found itself on the cutting edge of change.

Victoria's response was one based on tradition. Many Victorians in the postwar period did not view lack of industry as a major problem. Rather, they pointed to the fact that in 1951 retail sales per capita were 2.3 times greater than the national average and about double the provincial average. They did not attribute this to a high local income—in fact it was below the provincial and only slightly above the national level. They did attribute it to a burgeoning tourist industry and agreed that this, not the industrial sector, required intensive cultivation. Building on pre-war developments, this group within Victoria's community worked to upgrade tourist attraction and facilities. As a result, by 1971 and again in 1981, the percentage of employment in tourist-related activities exceeded that in any other sector.

Public administration and defence also continued to provide a large amount of employment for Victorians. Although it was eclipsed in 1971 by the tourist sector as the city's largest employer, it nonetheless far exceeded provincial, national, and other western Canadian city levels. In fact in 1981 Ottawa was the only Canadian city that exceeded Victoria in percentage of employment in this area.

Perhaps the most significant new development in the general service/information employment category related to the founding of the University of Victoria in 1963. From an enrolment of 2,000 in 1963-1964, the university had expanded to some 9,000-10,000 full- and part-time students. The full-time students, over 60 percent of whom were from outside the Victoria region, spent some thirty million dollars annually in the local community. The university itself employed over 1,300 full-time and 700 part-time employees for a total salary expenditure of sixty-four million dollars. No firm or institution, other than the government, created more employment—direct and indirect—in the Victoria region.

This trend toward an increased percentage of employment in the general service/information field and to a lesser extent in government sectors paralleled activity in most other Canadian cities. Even the high technology component of information services began to slowly set down roots in Victoria in the early 1980s. Once again the city's economic behaviour differed not in direction, but in degree.

The same holds true for trends in income. It has often been noted that Victorians earn on a percentage basis more money from pension and general investments than do the citizens of any other Canadian city. Victorians take home less money on a percentage basis from wages and salaries than do citizens in any other Canadian city.

In one respect this certainly makes the island city unique. Of more significance, however, is the fact that the trend for income in both these areas in all major Canadian cities has followed Victoria.

Victoria's income pattern is tied to the age profile of its citizens. By 1981, 25.7 percent of its inhabitants were over the age of sixty-five with 19 percent over the age of seventy. It is not surprising then that retirement income—pensions and investments—bulked large. Nor can there be any doubt that Victoria is preeminently Canada's urban retirement center. Yet, once again, the rest of Canada is moving in Victoria's direction. The full implications of this trend have, of course, yet to be worked out. Victoria, with more than "a touch of grey," has the opportunity to be at the forefront of such explorations.

A second demographic trend that was widely paralleled elsewhere concerned the city's share of the total metropolitan population. Like Vancouver, Victoria's portion of the population has declined dramatically following the Second World War. In 1941 the city contained 59 percent of the metropolitan area's population. By 1981 the city's share had shrunk to 28 percent. And since 1966 the municipality of Saanich has contained more people than the city of Victoria. This trend had an important impact on the provision of services by Victoria to the outlying areas, for which the costs increased more quickly than the city's potential tax income. As a result Victoria continued to press for amalgamation, but probably in part because of the increasing size of their own population, the outlying municipalities, led by Saanich, opted for continued separation. While many intermunicipal arrangements emerged for the provision of medical, school, legal, library, and park services, formal amalgamation seemed to have few backers outside of Victoria.

Victoria had been concerned well before World War II about the usage of the city's facilities by people living in outlying areas who did not contribute to the central city's tax base. By the end of the 1950s, this problem had become especially acute due to the virtual exhaustion of vacant land suitable for development and added to the tax role. Mayor Richard Biggerstaff Wilson cautioned Victorians in January 1962 that the city had "very little room for building expansion within its boundaries . . . new projects . . . can only be paid for by an increase in taxation on existing property holders." Given the fact that about one-quarter of the city's assessment was tax exempt (church and government properties), residents already paid close to three-fifths of all land taxes. To demand more would not only have been socially and economically oppressive, it would have been politically unwise.

Yet seven years later, Mayor Hugh Stephen boasted

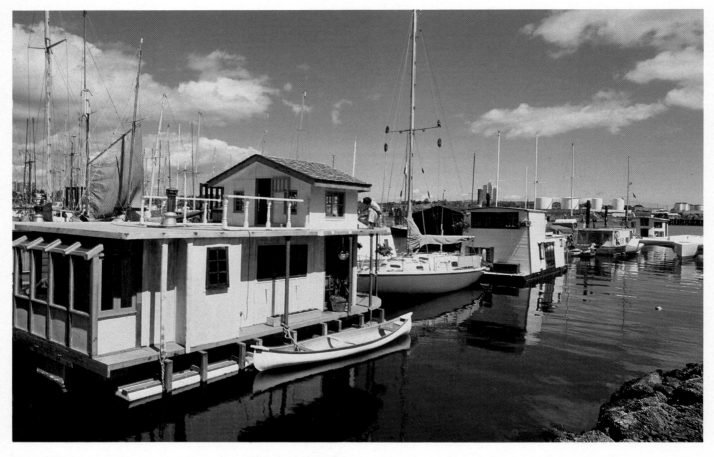

Above: *Fishing boats, houseboats, and pleasure craft co-exist at Fisherman's Wharf, a stone's throw from the inner harbour. Photo by Bob Garlick*

Left: *Hanging baskets, a city trademark, adorn a lamp standard on Douglas Street. Photo by Bob Garlick*

Facing page, top and bottom: *Victoria is very proud of its old homes, and a heritage programme has helped save many from redevelopment, although this programme is under increasing pressure due to declining municipal tax revenue. Photos by Bob Garlick*

in his inaugural address that sixty million dollars of development permits had been filed for since 1965, that the city's budget had increased by 2.85 million dollars since the mid-1960s, and that the mill rate had remained stable. Clearly Wilson's predictions had not proven correct. What, then, did take place?

As with so many other critical developments in the pre-World War II era, Victoria's situation was not unique. Central cities in other metropolitan areas faced similar dilemmas. In part because of this, in the 1960s lending institutions began to underwrite the construction of apartments and highrise office buildings. Amendments to the federal National Housing Act reflected the shift to multiple rather than single dwelling construction. By mid-1960, the era of urban renewal was in full tide.

This resulted in a massive shift in Victoria's physical character and residential space. Apartment development in Victoria during the 1960s outpaced the national average by 50 percent; by 1971 apartments represented 97 percent of all new housing construction in Victoria. In that decade apartment units for the first time outnumbered all other dwelling units in the city. The decade of the sixties also witnessed the transition from owner- to renter-occupied dwellings.

Older established neighbourhoods tended to be redeveloped first. James Bay, the oldest such neighbourhood in the city, received the highest priority. Between 1961 and 1966, developers erected 1,420 new apartment and townhouse units in that region. As late as 1984 James Bay contained fully one-quarter of all the city's apartment units—no other neighbourhood had more.

The redevelopment of James Bay and of other city neighbourhoods proceeded in the early years bereft of central planning. In its absence, zoning by-law amendments became the mechanism for urban change. Such a process reflected a fragmented perspective and carried with it the real dangers of creating a fragmented city. A more comprehensive perspective only began to emerge with the creation by the city in 1965 of an independent planning department responsible for overall change.

Even then the tendency of the city's planners and elected representatives was to ride rather than confront the winds of change. Not until late in 1967, for example, did a central plan receive council sanction for the renewal of James Bay. Even then it merely rubber-stamped what had already taken place. As David Tozer, a close student of that local improvement programme wrote, "it is hard to imagine a more blatant accommodation of the wishes of property developers and the high-rise residential form which the lending institutions were happiest to finance."

By 1970 reaction from within affected neighborhoods swiftly rose to the surface. Neighbourhood associations in Victoria, as in other Canadian cities, began to pressure city councils and demand the right to protect and create their own local space. In James Bay this resulted in the building of a community centre for seniors, and the development of an integrated community-run health, social, and educational programme. In founding the Health and Human Resources centre, James Bay and Victoria led Canada in the decentralization of control over essential services.

Referring to "the rape of James Bay," alderman and soon-to-be mayor Peter Pollen emerged in the early 1970s to champion neighbourhood rights. Others, some more radical, joined him. Similar to the situation in many Canadian cities, this blend of moderates and radicals, aided by a sputtering economy, were able to slow if not contain the renewal impulse throughout the 1970s.

The extent of redevelopment nevertheless had profound consequences and raised disturbing questions for Victoria's future. Destruction was the counterpart to renewal. In addition to the possible eradication of a neighbourhood's historic character and heritage, this process often carried with it the uprooting of individuals and families. City planners in Victoria and elsewhere had given little thought to the human dimension of urban upgrading and renewal. Brief consideration of three examples can serve to illustrate this tendency and to underline the complexity of issues raised by urban redevelopment in Victoria.

One hundred and fifty-seven households were displaced by a renewal scheme for the Rose-Blanshard region of the city in the late 1960s. The area did suffer from some "urban blight." In general the housing did require upgrading. Part of the plan, too, was to construct new low-cost rental accommodation. But the primary reason for dispossessing existing homeowners and razing the neighbourhood lay elsewhere. The minutes of a meeting of city planners on March 6, 1964, note:

... that the critical problem facing Victoria was not subsidized public housing or other aspects of the Urban Renewal Programme but rapid access to and adequate parking in the downtown core. Indeed, it was emphasized that if the city is to survive at all during the next forty years every effort must be made to combat the drift of commerce up the peninsula which will follow the inevitable northward movement of the population. It was felt, therefore, that the Blanshard access road is essential from the point of view of highway capacity, street alignment, and land use.

Given these priorities it is not surprising that those

who were dispossessed were dealt with in a too casual and uncaring fashion. The majority of those families subsisted on low incomes but little attention was given in the planning process for their relocation. In fact on the average they moved to dwellings that cost 40 percent more for less space. As Robert Robertson, the historian of the Rose-Blanshard programme, pointed out:

The city knew the whereabouts of less than 20 percent of the displaced households after relocation and, therefore, could not assure that the rest were rehoused in decent, safe, and sanitary accommodation at fair and reasonable rentals, as was required by the National Housing Act.

A second renewal programme raised issues of paramount importance to Victoria's future. Many of the poorest of the city's elderly people lived in the central business district in old hotels and rooming houses at moderate rents. They had lived there for a long period of time and had naturally built up strong community relationships. But the buildings were often in bad physical condition and stood as eyesores in the downtown tourist area. Almost invariably these buildings did not conform to new stringent fire safety regulations implemented in the mid-1970s. The fire marshal's solution was to tear them down. According to a study by Michael Sullivan some 400 inner city hotel rooms were "lost" by the end of the 1970s. Given the municipality's demographic profile, to provide for the well-being of the increasingly displaced elderly poor and preserve a sense of community for them while doing so is one of Victoria's most pressing current challenges and responsibilities.

After World War II, Victoria's Chinatown, a most historic and distinctive area, began to rapidly deteriorate. With the relaxation of anti-Chinese legislation, Chinatown residents gradually moved out into the wider community with the result that by the late 1970s only some 100 persons still resided within its shrinking boundaries. Labelled "the real slum area of Victoria" by city planners in 1964, the city nevertheless decided to exclude it from any general redevelopment plans. The hope seemed to be that it would disappear under its own inertia.

It nearly did. A poll of tourists in the late 1970s revealed that 80 percent had not even been aware that Victoria possessed a Chinatown. Only the spirited commitment of David Lai, a professor of geography at the University of Victoria, saved the area from total disintegration. Taking advantage of lessons learned from earlier development schemes, Victoria's Planning Department commissioned Lai to provide a survey of "views and

opinions" of local residents and property owners as to their desires for the area's future. This report emphasized the need to provide monies for facelifting, renovations, and, in some cases, the total rehabilitation of selected areas in Chinatown. But it went beyond beautification. As Lai commented, "Chinese people at present are apathetic, indifferent or doubtful about the future of Chinatown." To restore their faith, local residents had to be active in any renovation and redesign. A Chinese Community Centre which would attract young people and coordinate inter-association social functions became a centerpiece of Lai's recommendation. In the context of past redevelopment planning, this was an enlightened and sensible procedure. In the context of the history of Victoria's Chinese population, it remains to be seen whether it is simply a case of too little, too late.

One of Victoria's most cherished images is its reputation as a garden, park, and environmental paradise. Certainly the city inherited much splendour. But as noted previously Victoria's residents have had a tendency to passively accept their environment. This is especially true in the sense of assuming that no matter what they did, the natural beauty and resilience of their physical surroundings would compensate for it. As in other North American cities, the need for care, preservation, and environmental protection only slowly became apparent.

Take parks, for example. During the pre-World War I boom years the city's residents refused to underwrite the purchase of recreational and parkland and also refused to fund a permanent parks board. By 1947, while the city controlled ample parkland outside of its boundaries—Thetis Lake, Elk Lake, Goldstream, and Mount Douglas—"the area within the city," a local official claimed, "is low" compared to other cities. Especially lacking were neighbourhood playgrounds for children. Prior to 1956 no overall plan existed for such facilities and land reserved by one council for park use was often sold by a later council for other purposes. By the late 1960s, however, following increased pressure from local community groups, park development and preservation was included in a series of comprehensive plans for the city's development. By 1983 the city boasted forty-four neighbourhood playlots, playgrounds, and parks in addition to a series of "greens, squares, and ornamental areas." The city finally had earned its park-like image.

Despite the concern of the tourist lobby and more importantly, following 1970, of a variety of neighbourhood groups, Victoria's record concerning broader environmental issues has been surprisingly contentious. Beginning in the 1890s, the city officially sanctioned a longstanding informal practice of dumping garbage in the ocean. Mayor Percy Beale Scurrah defended this

Clockwise from top: *Victoria comes alive with the Swiftsure Classic.*
A lone sailboat catches the setting sun.
Chinatown features the Gate of Harmonious Interests.
Thunderbird Park celebrates the area's Indian heritage.
Photos by Bob Garlick

policy in 1956 by referring to the sea as a "bottomless pit." Three years later he had changed his mind. He told a local Kiwanis Club gathering:

As you know we have had complaints and very justifiable complaints for many years regarding the garbage returning to our beaches. . . . Only last year I was called out of my home one evening to look at Foul Bay. I went down and there were tens of thousands of tin cans, bits of orange and grapefruit and all the assorted material that goes into our garbage can on the Foul Bay Beach.

He had it cleaned up and instituted a system of landfill sites as an alternative to ocean dumping.

However, the concept of a "bottomless pit" still governs Victoria's disposal of raw sewage. Pleading that experts are divided as to whether or not the dumping of untreated sewage into the ocean constitutes "a health hazard," city authorities have consistently adopted the position that "when and if new knowledge becomes available we can always then add the required amount of treatment." Obviously Victoria's traditional passivity with regard to environmental protection has yet to be completely eradicated.

Victoria has always had potential; the problem has been one of definition, not one of stunted possibilities. In a commercial seaward-looking era, Victoria rose to become an important regional entrepot. In an industrial era Victoria did not fit, other than as a respite from the mainstream. Too often manipulated by land developers and too often inexcusably callous toward non-white people, the city has much to atone for.

For other than brief periods in its history, Victoria has been viewed as a comfortable perch on a rim remote from change. This makes it very difficult to appreciate the fact that in important ways this is no longer—and in some senses never was—the case. With regard to several central economic and social trends, Victoria has moved from that remote rim to the cutting edge. A new era dominated by information services, an aging population, the search for leisure and recreation, and an emerging Pacific orientation, offers great possibilities for the future of this island spot. Its major characteristics fit it well for a leadership role in the post-industrial world. It remains to be seen whether it has the collective will to perform that role. If it does, the future may well be Victoria's "cup of tea."

Partners in Progress

By G.E. Mortimore

In the last years of the twentieth century, British Columbia's island capital city is moving into the commercial mainstream after a period of stagnation. This is a new growth phase in an economy that has registered massive growth while alternating from boom to depression since pre-European times.

In the mid-nineteenth century a strategic position between fertile land and a good sea harbour made Victoria the largest city on the Pacific Coast north of San Francisco. Its importance as a European colonial centre began when the Hudson's Bay Company built a trading fort among the Llekwungen, or Sea-Smell People, a division of the Straits Salish.

Victoria's population and commerce made a spectacular advance when the city became the main entry port for the Fraser River gold mines. As placer mining by frontier adventurers was succeeded by industrial mining with expensive machinery, and as immigrants flowed in, pushed native people off the land, and replaced the native system of regional trade and regional raiding warfare with the emerging European system of world trade and world wars, there were several swings between boom and slump; yet Victoria grew as a manufacturing, export-import, and distributing centre. The sea was still the major highway, but the railroad was coming.

Victoria lost its fight for continued dominance when a plan for a sea bridge and Victoria rail terminus was rejected. The Canadian Pacific Railway guaranteed the rise of Vancouver and the eclipse of Victoria. The eclipse did not happen immediately. For a time Victoria expanded as a seaport and as a centre for the manufacture of chemicals, soap, paint, roofing material, flour, canned food, wine, machinery, and wood products.

However, most of the factories drifted away. Tourism, government payrolls, and pensions became the main sources of income. Then the tide turned. Transportation made the difference. In the 1980s Victoria is served by dozens of daily flights and ferries. It supplies world markets with electronic equipment, oceanographic instruments, research services, computer services, robotics, plastics, inflatable boats, large fibreglass yachts, and high-technology ships.

Faced by the industrializing cheap-labour countries of Asia, Victoria is starting to build a future on resources plus invention. Trees were squandered by wasteful harvesting and scanty replanting and exported in raw or lightly finished form as logs and lumber. Now they will be intensely conserved and exported in many forms, from chopsticks to prefabricated houses. Invention will produce a changing stream of products and services, from high-quality local food crops to computer software, from targeted tourism to the export of entire factories to produce B.C.-designed ferries or machinery for mining, logging, fish farming, natural-gas propulsion, mini-hydro, pollution control, and waste recycling.

Today political leaders accept the need for a blend of government action and private enterprise in remaking the economy. Victoria-based entrepreneurs, including those who are represented in this book and who have chosen to support this project, will continue to prosper as they have done before—by adapting efficiently to changing markets. The process of building a new economy for the twenty-first century is under way.

CHAPTER VI

This circa 1860 view of Yates Street looking toward the harbour was painted by Sarah Crease. The bank on the left is the Bank of British North America, the first in Victoria. The druggist sign hangs over Moore Company druggist on the corner of Langley Street. (PABC)

GREATER VICTORIA CIVIC ARCHIVES SOCIETY

An alarm call to warn of an impending act of vandalism reached Victoria archivist Ainslie Helmcken on the afternoon of Halloween, 1967.

"We've got orders from the municipal manager to clean out all the papers from the vault and put them on the Halloween bonfire for the kids," an Oak Bay municipal truck driver told him.

In 1986 Helmcken recalled his attempt to save the documents: "I grabbed four boxes from the bonfire and ran away with them before anyone could start asking questions. They contained all the information about the incorporation of Oak Bay, the first elections and the first assessments.

"We still have that material in the city archives. There must have been a couple of hundred more boxes on the bonfire, ready to burn. I couldn't get anybody to listen to me about the value of the stuff. So they burned the rest of it that night."

Even after Helmcken had retired as archivist, such horror stories were one of his favorite topics.

At one time Victoria's old civic documents were routinely shovelled into a truck and sent to the Sidney Roofing and Paper Co. plant, where they were recycled as roofing material. "There's more history in the roofs of Victoria than there is in the history books," Helmcken says.

Helmcken, a great-grandson of Governor James Douglas, had a career in business, law, and public service behind him when he started the Victoria City Archives in 1966 at the age of 66. The idea came from Mayor Alf Toone, who asked him to sort through the city's masses of old records and make some recommendations for putting them in order.

After Helmcken had made his report, Mayor Toone surprised him by asking when he wanted to start work as archivist. He agreed to hold the post for three years, until the city

could find someone else. In reality he stayed for 18 years, and retired with the honor of Freeman of the City.

Helmcken organized the Greater Victoria Civic Archives Society in 1977. He had been asked to help document Victoria's surviving heritage buildings. This project stirred him to reach out for allies and helpers. He knew there was a large body of public opinion in favor of conserving historical artifacts and the documentary raw material of history, and he believed that the time had come to mobilize that sentiment for action.

The society was launched in February 1977, and officially chartered in March. Its aims were to encourage the collection and preservation of historically significant records, to foster awareness of archives material and access to it in public archives, to promote systems of records management,

---

Ainslie Helmcken, founder of Victoria's city archives and Greater Victoria Civic Archives Society. Helmcken's grandfather was Dr. J.D. Helmcken, a son-in-law of Sir James Douglas, first governor of Vancouver Island and British Columbia. Curtis Studio photograph by Curtis Lantinga

and to encourage the production of books, articles, and audiovisual material of merit.

"Ideally, the archives is a working department of government in municipalities, provinces, and at the federal level," says Brian Tobin, president of the Greater Victoria Civic Archives Society and former editor of *The Victoria Daily Times.* A committee that includes the archivist and department heads should decide at intervals which documents are to be thrown out and which are to be kept.

In 1986 the ongoing major project of the society, in collaboration with the city, was to mark the positions of the stockade, gate, and northeast bastion of the fort with a double line of toughened wear-resistant bricks set into the sidewalk of Government Street and the lane leading to Bastion Square. Each brick is inscribed with the name of a nineteenth-century or early twentieth-century resident, including Hudson's Bay people and Indians who signed the Fort Victoria treaty.

Another ongoing project is the campaign to get more space for the city archives.

McGILL AND ORME, LTD.

"The doctors ask us to open pharmacies in their buildings. They want clinic pharmacies that specialize in total health care—not miniature department stores."

The professional strategy of McGill and Orme, Ltd., is summed up in that statement by R. Bedford Bates, who became president and part-owner in 1973, after 20 years as a working pharmacist. He was explaining why most of the company's operations are in medical buildings. The trend began in 1956 with the Medical Arts Building at the corner of Cook Street and Pandora Avenue. It continued as other medical centres arose.

This hometown group of pharmacies has grown to its present size by systematically assembling a network of personal relations and service to both doctors and patients.

When C.H. Orme of Prince Rupert, British Columbia, sent his partner and former employee, W.W. McGill, to open a prescriptions-only pharmacy at 629 1/2 Fort Street, Victoria, in 1930, the pattern of close co-operation wth doctors was established from the start. The first professional colleague "Mac" McGill hired was Harold Davenport, chief pharmacist at St. Joseph's Hospital. McGill took Davenport on staff because he knew all the doctors.

Orme continued to operate his drugstore in Prince Rupert, while McGill managed the Victoria store. Two pharmacists and a delivery boy were the whole labor force. Growth of McGill and Orme was relatively slow until the 1960s, when the com-

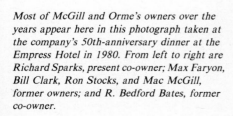

W.W. "Mac" McGill in heritage drug store at Victoria's Provincial Museum, equipped and furnished under the direction of Mr. and Mrs. R. Bedford Bates, with McGill as consultant. McGill and Orme donated many of the artifacts here and some of those in a nineteenth-century drug store at Barkerville, British Columbia.

pany began buying general drugstores, closing them, and hiring each proprietor-pharmacist (with his list of clients and his prescription files) to staff an expanding organization.

Today McGill and Orme has nine pharmacies and one surgical supply store. Eight of the pharmacies are in medical buildings, and all the outlets are in Victoria. Bates and Richard W. Sparks, who were co-owners until 1986, turned down opportunities to expand into other cities. They wanted all of their facilities within easy visiting distance. Bates sold his share in

McGill and Orme to Sparks and Ralph Storey on February 28, 1986, but he continues to take a personal interest in the company.

The show globes of colored fluids in the Fort Street store, eight doors east of the original location, are a symbolic link with the time when medicinal tinctures were kept in the forefront. The one-bicycle delivery service has grown into a delivery fleet of seven motor vehicles. In the 1930s the establishment sometimes bartered medicine for fruit and vegetables. Now the firm's sales are $7 million per year; the payroll is $1.6 million for 80 employees.

Orme left the business in 1942. McGill sold his interest in 1956 and stayed on as an employee. By mid-1986, at age 96, he was still working three days a week in the department where special ointments, tinctures, and elixirs were made under his supervision. The career of Canada's oldest practising pharmacist began when all prescriptions were compounded by hand. It continues in the age of computer co-ordinated prescriptions, when 75 percent of drugs are prepackaged.

McGill and Orme's computer system, the first of its kind in Victoria, keeps each client's pharmaceutical history, warns of any harmful combinations of drugs, and relieves pharmacists of paperwork—allowing them time for personal consultation with patients and doctors.

Most of McGill and Orme's owners over the years appear here in this photograph taken at the company's 50th-anniversary dinner at the Empress Hotel in 1980. From left to right are Richard Sparks, present co-owner; Max Faryon, Bill Clark, Ron Stocks, and Mac McGill, former owners; and R. Bedford Bates, former co-owner.

ISLAND FARMS DAIRY

Door-to-door delivery by the Island Farms milkman continues today after a dairy revolution that has sent glass bottles and cans to the museum of commercial antiques, and has replaced them with cartons and refrigerated stainless-steel tanks.

The milkman's job has changed. He now calls at houses only two days a week instead of seven; and doorstep delivery contributes only 20 percent of the sales volume at Island Farms Dairies Co-operative Association, instead of 100 percent. However, the tradition of personal service is so strongly established that it will endure into the twenty-first century.

The days of horse-drawn milk wagons are gone, and today milk is picked up at farms in stainless-steel tank trucks, but Island Farms is still farmer-owned and delivers directly to the customer's door.

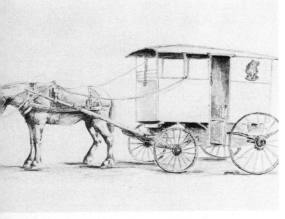

This is the opinion of Fred Mockford, who started as a wartime horse-and-cart milk delivery boy in 1943, and became general manager of Island Farms in 1983. The same view is held by marketing manager Gordon Ganong—a member of the new generation of business executives co-ordinating the distribution of 350 different kinds, flavors, and sizes of Island Farms products, from yogurt and cottage cheese to ice cream and orange juice.

In an age when dairy farming has been concentrated into a large-scale specialized agribusiness, and the dairy trade has expanded into the processing and sale of a wide variety of foods, Island Farms trucks in their uniform of green and white sprinkled with multicolored daisies still go on their rounds, to neighborhood stores and homes, restaurants, and modern supermarkets.

The company began as The Registered Jersey Dairies in 1932, but in its growth it has absorbed other dairies—which in turn were compounded from earlier dairies with origins extending back to 1911. Island Farms' history is like a river with many tributary streams.

When George Malcolm and his brother-in-law, Albert Doney, began selling milk as The Registered Jersey Dairies, there were drivers from dozens of rival ventures leaving quarts and pints on city doorsteps. Malcolm bottled the milk on the family farm on Mount Newton Cross Road; Doney delivered it.

By 1935 the number of dairies on southern Vancouver Island had reached a peak of 140. Over the years there have been 300—or even more, if history is traced back to all the mixed-farm operators who carried milk in cans and poured it into the householders' jugs.

Demand for premium-quality Jersey milk in the 1930s soon outran the supply. Other farmers joined the group of Registered Jersey shareholders. In 1936 the bottling operation moved to the old Tod fish-packing plant on Broughton Street, where the first pasteurizing vats were installed. Massive changes in the dairy industry were beginning. More money was needed to equip larger farms and larger processing plants with increasingly safe, sanitary, and efficient machinery to serve a growing and changing market.

Registered Jersey Dairies could not raise enough capital. In 1942 the farmer/owners sold to a group of Vancouver businessmen, who incorporated as Island Farms Ltd., and they in turn reached the limit of their willingness to invest. A newly organized producer co-op, Island Farms Dairies Co-operative Association, purchased the dairy company's inadequate plant in 1944—and gradually saved and borrowed enough money to put it through a series of moves, enlargements, and modernizations. Since 1964 John Pendray has been president of Island Farms; over the past 22 years he has been a major force in the dairy's development.

Economic pressures triggered many other amalgamations and buyouts. By 1967 the number of Victoria-based dairies had shrunk to six. Now Island Farms is the only surviving full-service dairy that delivers to local homes.

There are 175 employees and 85 vehicles working out of the 15,000-square-foot plant on Dowler Place and the Chemainus subdepot. The production and market area is Vancouver Island from Parksville south. Half the milk comes from the Cowichan Valley; most of it is sold in Victoria. The dairy's board of directors, six in total, are elected from the 52 farmer/members who own Island Farms. That number is only half the membership held in the peak years of small farms—1940s—but the volume of milk has increased tenfold.

PEMBERTON HOUSTON WILLOUGHBY

Pemberton Houston Willoughby, Western Canada's largest regional investment company, began in Victoria in 1887 as the two-man firm of Pemberton & Son, surveyors, civil engineers, estate agents, and financial agents.

Joseph Despard Pemberton, Vancouver Island's first colonial surveyor-general, was an Irish-born civil engineer who had built railways in England and Ireland. He came to Vancouver Island in 1851 and made his mark on history: He surveyed southern Vancouver Island for the first detailed maps, laid out the first Victoria townsite, designed and built public buildings, and sat as a member of the colonial legislature and council.

He started the family firm when he was 66 years old as a career inheritance for his son, Frederick Bernard Pemberton, who had just graduated as an engineer at the age of 22. Over the years investments and real estate became increasingly important in the work of Pemberton & Son, supplanting surveying and engineering.

F.B. Pemberton, who had become head of the firm after his father's death in 1893, established a Vancouver branch at 314 Homer Street in 1910. Pemberton & Son had funnelled in $13 million in mortgage funds, most of it from British investors, to finance the residential and commercial growth of Victoria and Vancouver.

In 1925 a group of Vancouver businessmen, which included Stanley Burke and Larry P. Smith, purchased the Vancouver operations, and in 1929 their business was divided into three Vancouver-based companies: Pemberton Realty, Pemberton Insurance and Pemberton & Son, and Vancouver Ltd., which dealt in stocks and bonds and was moved to 418 Howe Street.

In 1943 Pemberton & Son, Vancouver, became Pemberton Securities Corporation, Ltd., a name it was to keep until 1983. From the late 1930s onward the only links between the Vancouver-based firm and the Victoria-based company were friendship and shared history.

In 1974 Pemberton Securities Corporation, Ltd., merged with Ryan Investments of Vancouver. Its merger in February 1983 with the 58-year-old Saskatchewan firm of Houston Willoughby made the renamed firm of Pemberton Houston Willoughby the largest broker in Western Canada.

By 1986, the year before its 100th birthday, Pemberton Houston Willoughby was a Vancouver-based investment company that mobilized capital and handled investments worth hundreds of millions of dollars for corporations, governments, and individuals. It was a member of the Toronto, Montreal, Alberta, and Vancouver stock exchanges. Its 650 employees worked from 22 offices in

---

This two-storey building at the corner of Fort and Broad streets was the home of Pemberton and Son, which was the precursor of Pemberton Houston Willoughby. The structure burned down in 1908 and was replaced by the six-storey Pemberton Building, which was later sold to shipbuilder Norman Yarrow to then become the Yarrow Building.

British Columbia, Alberta, Saskatchewan, and Toronto.

The 10th-floor Victoria office at 747 Fort Street is a block away from the site of the first downtown office of Pemberton & Son, at the corner of Fort and Broad streets.

Chairman W. Robert Wyman, president Fred R. Wright, the 26 directors and the staff of managers, research analysts, traders, investment advisors, and planners pursue a strategy that they describe as innovative yet conservative. Covering the full spectrum of Canadian and U.S. securities, they focus especially on the resource-based industries of the West. "We specialize in investment-grade securities, top-quality people, and professional research," Wright explains.

Ample chances for personal development, plus the company's open communication style, earned Pemberton a place in *The Financial Post*'s book, *The Top 100 Companies to Work for in Canada.*

Pemberton stock was held entirely by management and staff shareholders until 1986, when the company sold shares to the public to increase its capital. After-tax returns varying between 20 and 165 percent on staff-held stock point toward the success of the Pemberton investment strategy.

PEMBERTON, HOLMES LTD.

"People told great-grandfather that he was building his house much too far from town," says Philip Holmes, president of Pemberton, Holmes Ltd.

His great-grandfather was Joseph Despard Pemberton, first surveyor for the Hudson's Bay Company on Vancouver Island, first surveyor-general, and founder of the Victoria-based family-owned real estate, insurance, mortgage, and appraisal company that celebrates its 100th birthday in 1987.

The house too far from town was "Gonzales," the 20-room mansion that J.D. Pemberton built in 1885 among fields and oak trees at one corner of his 1,200-acre farm. The city grew far beyond it and swallowed the farm and then the house itself. "Gonzales" stood for 67 years at the site that became the corner of St. Charles Street and Rockland Avenue, 20 minutes' walk or five minutes' drive from the Inner Harbour.

"JDP" had built his house in a view location, showing foresight to invest in land when it was inexpensive. Planning vision has been a major characteristic down the generations in the firm that is now known as Pemberton, Holmes Ltd., which took shape as a federation of two families joined together in business and in marriage.

The Pemberton and Holmes coats of arms, and four of the family portraits, hang on the panelled stairway wall in the company's building at the corner of Government and Broughton streets, on the spot where a vegetable garden used to grow at the southeast corner of the log stockade of the Hudson's Bay Company's fort.

The first face on the wall is that of J.D. Pemberton, who arrived at Fort Victoria in 1851 at age 30 by canoe on the final stage of a three-month sea-and-land journey from Great Britain. As a grandson of a Lord Mayor of Dublin, he inherited a tradition of high achievement. Soon af-

Philip Despard Pemberton "Pip" Holmes, DFC, CD, KLJ, FRI, RI(BC), president of Pemberton, Holmes Ltd.

ter graduation as a civil engineer from Trinity College, Dublin, the young man built railways in Ireland and England. On Vancouver Island he made the surveys for the first detailed maps, and was responsible for laying out the first townsite of Victoria. He planned and built the colony's roads, bridges, and public buildings, and prospected the Nanaimo coalfields.

At first he lived in the fort, then Pemberton later purchased a 20- by 30-foot log house with barn, outhouses, and "five acres of enclosed tilled land." After his marriage in 1864 he left government service to devote himself to business and agriculture, at the same time sitting in the first legislative assembly, and becoming a leader in the social and commercial life of Victoria. He enlarged his lands until they included

most of what is now southern Oak Bay and eastern Rockland Avenue-Fairfield.

The enterprising landowner was 66 when he and his eldest son, Frederick Bernard Pemberton, formed the partnership of Pemberton & Son—estate and financial agents, surveyors, and civil engineers. "FBP" had just graduated as a civil and mechanical engineer from University College, London. "JDP" underwrote the security of the business with his estate, derived from early colonial days when the European population was small and the Hudson's Bay Company was under pressure to sell land at low prices and bring in settlers. Later, as the population grew and prices rose, the estate was carved off piece by piece to provide for children and raise money for the business.

In 1887 the Pembertons ran the business from "Gonzales." In the following year they set up an office in a building at the corner of Fort and Broad streets. "JDP" had earlier chosen this property rather than another because it included a stable for his horse. He died of a heart attack at age 72 when he was riding across country on a Hunt Club paperchase.

The second face on the wall is that of F.B. Pemberton, who guided the firm through cycles of boom and depression, and kept it afloat through the difficult years of the 1914-1918 war.

"FBP" was a man of many skills: engineer, businessman, athlete, agriculturist, horticulturist. He imported and commercially grew the first holly on Vancouver Island.

Mortgages, insurance, and property management fees provided most of the firm's revenue in its first half-century. Much of the mortgage money that financed the growth of Victoria and Vancouver flowed in from lenders in Britain, through Pemberton & Son and its British connection.

Pemberton & Son rebuilt and extended its building at Fort and Broad streets in 1907, but it was destroyed by fire two years later. "FBP" designed and built a six-story structure on the same site. In the 1940s it was sold to Norman Yarrow, and has been known since as the Yarrow Building. The business then moved to its present headquarters.

The third face on the wall is that of Major Henry Cuthbert Holmes, an Oxford M.A., barrister of the Middle Temple in London, former officer in the Irish Guards, and son of an Indian Civil Service judge. He married F.B. Pemberton's second daughter, Philippa, and went to work in 1921 for Pemberton & Son, becoming president of the firm in 1933.

The business was incorporated in 1943 as Pemberton, Holmes Ltd. The new name recognized Holmes' part in building the public confidence that enabled the company to continue as Vancouver Island's largest (in residential listings) and best-known real estate firm. Through a network of relatives, friends, and business associates, Holmes mobilized increasing amounts of mortgage capital plus financing to buy out the investors who had helped the firm through the 1930s Depression. He was also cofounder of Brentwood College School.

The contemporary face on the wall

is that of Holmes' son, squadron leader Philip Despard Pemberton "Pip" Holmes, DFC, who joined the organization in 1945 after a distinguished career with an RCAF bomber command in Europe, and became president in 1965. During his tenure the company has entered its most vigorous period of growth. The volume of business increased from $6.5 million to $40 million in 16 years. Currently there is a staff of 75 working from three offices—in Victoria, Sidney, and Ganges. Philip Holmes' daughter, Diana Holmes, and his nephew, Richard Holmes, work for the firm. His cousin, also named Philip Holmes, heads the Sidney company.

The private business vision of the Pemberton-Holmes family has been matched by its public planning imagination. Before Canada or the Canadian Pacific Railway existed, "JDP" published a plan for a "British emigrant and postal route" by wagon road and waterway across northern North America. "FBP" played a leading part in creating the municipality of Oak Bay; he recommended

Three generations in the combined Pemberton-Holmes family business, which marks its centenary in 1987 (from left): J.D. Pemberton, F.B. Pemberton, and Major H. Cuthbert Holmes.

that the big trees of Cathedral Grove be preserved, sacrificed development profits, and sold land for Victoria Golf Club at a relatively low price, to keep it as a green space.

Cuthbert and Philip Holmes headed Victoria's Chamber of Commerce and Real Estate Board in father-son succession. They campaigned together and individually for regional planning, public waterfront walkways, highway greenbelts, and extensive park space.

Philip Holmes has been honorary aide-de-camp to three lieutenant-governors, chairman of the Provincial Capital Commission, and vice-chairman of the University of Victoria's Board of Governors. He was the only Canadian to be elected president of the International Real Estate Federation, based in Paris. In his two-year term he visited 44 countries. His ideal is that every family in the world should own an adequate dwelling—an ideal that, if realized, would pay off in work for millions of artisans and producers of building materials.

Major Cuthbert Holmes envisioned a developed Vancouver Island of small cities and quiet commercial-industrial parks among forests and gardens. "Climatically and geographically Vancouver Island is unique in Canada," he said. "The Island is the size of many a nation, such as Belgium, Switzerland, and Denmark, and just as strategically located for trade. Therefore the Island should and can expect to support a population approximately that of those nations." Made a Freeman of the city, he died in 1968 at which time *The Victoria Daily Times* commented: "Many of the major concepts which have been embraced in Greater Victoria's commercial and recreational life or are now being actively contemplated were foreseen and urged by Major Holmes long before the community was ready to accept them."

VICTORIA'S OGDEN POINT DOCKS OPERATED BY WESTCAN TERMINALS LTD.

Victoria's Outer Harbour was in danger of falling into disuse when Hector Campbell turned its fortunes around.

The story began when the federal government built a 2,500-foot breakwater and two 1,000-foot piers at Ogden Point in 1913-1915 to receive an expected massive increase in sea trade from the Panama Canal, which was built at the same time. Victoria was the nearest Canadian port to the Panama. It seemed likely to become a major manufacturing centre and cargo terminal.

In fact, the increase in trade was moderate and temporary. The port was in a slump when Hector Campbell founded Western Lumber Carriers (forerunner of Westcan) in 1946 and established Ogden Point as a viable deep-sea terminal.

With the support of Major-General G.R. Pearkes, V.C., M.P., he persuaded the C.N.R., who held an en-

trustment to Ogden Point Docks, to build an improved storage area and assembly yard. By the early 1950s the port was booming as some 50 small lumber and plywood mills utilized Ogden Point to ship their products to world markets. Competitive pressure from larger firms later forced most of the smaller mills to close. Campbell, always a resourceful cargo entrepreneur, moved to counter this loss of business by trucking cargo from up-island points, and by barging other cargo from Vancouver, the Olympic Peninsula in Washington State, and even Alaska.

Changes in marine, harbour, and manufacturing technology perpetuated a trend to larger and more specialized ships. Huge cargo ships with containerized cargoes became the norm. Small cargoes and part-cargoes went out of style, and Victoria lost its place as a sizable cargo seaport.

When the Ogden Point warehouse burned down in 1977, Campbell led a campaign to build the present 100,000-square-foot warehouse, with facilities for cruise ship passengers. Cruise vessel traffic increased from 12 cruise ship stopovers with 4,300 passengers in 1969 to 78 ships and

Hector Campbell, the cargo entrepreneur who founded the Westcan companies.

90,000 passengers in 1986.

Hector Campbell, with his vice-presidents, George Robbins and Gerry Lutz, purchased the Westcan companies in July 1985. Hector died on December 17, 1985, but not before he realized that the cruise vessel business could help make Victoria the tourist capital of the Pacific Northwest. The Ogden Point docks are near the heart of the city, where visitors can reach most tourist attractions by a short walk. Victoria's geography allows people to compress an array of experiences into a brief visit. Close-in attractions range from modern restaurants to a nineteenth-century castle, undersea aquarium, indoor tropical gardens, and galleries of West Coast arts and gifts. For more distant attractions such as Butchart's Gardens, buses, taxis, or rental cars meet the ships at dockside.

Robbins and Lutz are reaching out for more cargoes and additional tourist-related business. Meanwhile, Westcan people work to make cruise vessel visitors feel welcome.

Victoria's outer harbour in 1954. Lower left, the old Rithet piers, at that time occupied by Victoria machinery depot shipyard, since taken over by the Coast Guard. Right, the old grain elevator, since demolished. Foreground, steamship Princess Marguerite, then sailing under colours of Canadian Pacific.

TIMES-COLONIST

"Printing is the oldest of the industrial processes. It has confronted technical change on a major scale roughly once in a century since the Renaissance, when moving type was introduced in Europe."

- Anthony Smith, in "Goodbye Gutenberg: The Newspaper Revolution of the 1980's."

Two Victoria newspapers that competed for nearly a century are combined in the *Times-Colonist,* Canada's oldest newspaper west of Ontario.

The Daily Colonist was 122 years old and *The Victoria Daily Times* was 96 when rising costs and the logic of the new computer technology compelled them to merge in 1980 to form a newspaper that was larger and more efficient than either of its parents.

That was the latest chapter in a story that began when Amor De Cosmos printed the first issue of the weekly *British Colonist* in a leaky shed on Wharf Street on December 11, 1858. He sold 200 copies. By 1986 the *Times-Colonist* had an average seven-days-a-week circulation of 80,000 a day.

Each ancestor of the *Times-Colonist* began publication at a time of economic upheaval and social change. Each represented a step in the progress of newspaper technology.

The British Colonist began when Victoria was a tent-and-shack boom town in the first year of the Fraser River gold rush. It was printed on a 100-year-old French press, and its antique type was hand set from handwritten copy.

The Victoria Daily Times began in the period that historian Margaret Ormsby labelled "The Great Potlatch." Victoria was experiencing a construction boom. Railways were being built, and land, timber, and minerals were handed out at bargain

Amor De Cosmos, a black-bearded political swashbuckler, who came from Nova Scotia via the California gold fields, started the British Colonist *in this building, which he owned. Artist's rendering by Barry F. King*

prices.

The nineteenth-century mechanical transformation of printing was under way when the first issue of *The Times* was printed on a power-driven, flat-bed press on June 9, 1884. Victoria would soon have the whole array of hot-metal technology, from Mergenthaler's new linotype to stereotypers making massive plates for a high-speed rotary press.

When the combined *Times-Colonist* appeared on September 2, 1980, the plant had already gone through its twentieth-century change. The publications had moved under the same roof in 1951, and had progressively shared one department after another until only editorial staffs were separate. During that period the ponderous hot-metal system gave way to a fast, lightweight process by which computer-prepared, pasted-up "cold" type was photographed on paper and transferred to the press on a plastic plate. It was the greatest advance in printing technology since movable

type.

The *Times-Colonist,* now owned by Canadian Newspapers Company Limited, a subsidiary of The Thomson Newspapers Ltd., and managed by publisher Colin D. McCullough, has outlived or absorbed more than 20 rivals. It has earned a distinguished reputation for public service. *The Colonist* and De Cosmos did much to win responsible government and negotiate British Columbia's stormy entry into Confederation. Many *Times* and *Colonist* editors, publishers, and owners have achieved power and fame. On the *Colonist* side, De Cosmos and John Robson became B.C. premiers: James Dunsmuir was premier and lieutenant-governor; David W. Higgins became Speaker of the Legislature. On the *Times* side were Premier Robert Beaven and Mayor John Grant, who were co-founders; Senator William Templeman; and Speaker Nancy Hodges. *Times* editors Benjamin Nicholas and Bruce Hutchison, among others, earned places of honor in the annals of journalism and politics.

Colonist founder De Cosmos and Governor James Douglas, each of whom was a nation-builder in his own style, were political enemies. In 1859 De Cosmos won a battle for press freedom when Douglas tacked a proclamation on the wall of the Hudson's Bay fort forbidding publication of *The Colonist* until an L800 bond had been posted. Citizens subscribed the money.

In 1980 *The Times* and cartoonist Bob Bierman won another battle about a cartoon that depicted then Human Resources Minister Bill Vander Zalm pulling wings off a fly, to symbolize his tough attitude toward native Indians and welfare recipients. Vander Zalm won a $3,500 libel judgement in B.C. Supreme Court, but B.C. Court of Appeal ruled in a landmark decision that the cartoon was fair political comment.

B.C. TEL

"Mr. Watson, come here, I want you."
-Alexander Graham Bell
Boston, 1876
"Send three boxes of Double Crown soap to Mr. Manette."
-Victoria and Esquimalt Telephone Company, Limited
Victoria, British Columbia, 1880

These two commands, separated by four years and 4,000 miles, signalled the start of worldwide telephone communication and British Columbia's role in its development.

In 1876 Alexander Graham Bell made his historic telephone call.

In 1880 the order for soap was the first message to pass over test lines linking two customers of the Victoria and Esquimalt Telephone Company, Limited, British Columbia's first telephone operation. The message travelled 600 yards from W.J. Jeffree's clothing store to the British Columbia Soap Works, which was owned by Jeffree's nephew, William J. Pendray.

W.J. Jeffree and the soap works

were the first customers. Two years earlier, however, demonstration lines had been hooked up between *The Daily Colonist's* office and the Canadian Pacific Railway's survey office some blocks away. *The Colonist* called the telephone a "curious little transmitter."

The newspaper continued, "Scores visited the editor's office yesterday, and all went away amazed and instructed."

People thought the telephone was an interesting novelty, but they took some time to accept it as a working instrument of communication. Victoria's first shipment of telephones remained in storage for nearly two years.

The Victoria and Esquimalt Telephone Company was organized by

---

British Columbia's first telephone poles, on Government Street, Victoria, in 1880. The photograph shows Government Street from Yates Street southward.

Robert Burns McMicking and Edgar Crow Baker. It began service in 1880 with 46 customers, each paying three dollars per month.

In 1904, through mergers and name changes, the enterprise became a part of the British Columbia Telephone Company—forerunner of B.C. Tel, which today serves virtually all of the province.

The city of Victoria has marked many "firsts" in telephone development in British Columbia. Among them have been the first advertisements for telephone service, the first political arguments centring on the telephone system, and British Columbia's first use of a series of new technological devices.

In early advertising, McMicking promoted the telephone as a service that would "transmit all languages with equal facility."

When McMicking was placing 70-foot-tall poles above Victoria streets to carry phone lines well clear of streetcar wires, Amor de Cosmos—

Colquitz Central Office men in Victoria (from left): Garry Greene and Malcolm Marsh.

who had been premier of British Columbia—complained about the one in front of his Government Street property. The city council of the day supported his objection, but reversed its vote in the face of rumours that the decision would close the phone system.

The Victoria telephone office moved several times as it grew: to the Five Sisters block on Government at Fort; then the Green Block on Broad; then, in 1912, to the present site of the main Victoria exchange at Blanshard and Yates.

That was the central location in the next telephone development in which Victoria led the province. In 1930 the manual switchboard was replaced by British Columbia's first automatic dial telephone exchange.

The conversion was complex, but it was accomplished with military precision and without interruption, owing to meticulous planning by James Hamilton, a former army major. The exchange required 135 tons of equipment; 17,000 telephones had to be changed, and customers had to be educated in how to use the new dial phones.

Robert McMicking's widow took part in the cutover ceremonies on November 1, 1930.

Victoria was in the lead again in 1979, when the electromechanical dial switching system was replaced

by electronic facilities—which were in place when B.C. Tel marked the centenary of the Victoria and Esquimalt Telephone Company in 1980. Three generations of McMicking's family were special guests at the celebrations at the Yates Street office.

In 1981, without public fanfare, B.C. Tel placed its first operational fibre-optic cable—which combines hair-thin glass strands with laser light to create high-quality transmission—in the Victoria system. It links the downtown exchange and the South Hill radio transmission site.

In 1985 the Belmont, Colquitz, and Sidney offices were converted to digital technology, which converts voice, data, and image into digits; transmits them at incredible speed and safe from electrical interference; then reconstitutes them to their original form. More digital conversions are scheduled in the years ahead.

Today the Greater Victoria area has 15 exchange offices, most of which are served by electronic switches. They link 145,248 telephones and serve voice, data, and image requirements of residential and business customers.

The city also serves as the administrative headquarters for B.C. Tel's Island Area, which covers all Vancouver Island and parts of the mainland coast, including Powell River.

Victoria is the focal point of Provnet, the largest single project ever undertaken by B.C. Tel for one customer. The final switching centre in Provnet was put into service in September 1985, completing a two-year endeavour that created a private telecommunications network for the British Columbia government.

Provnet has eight switching centres and links 45 government offices throughout the province on a direct-line basis, providing the full range of modern telecommunication services required today for effective administration and service to the public.

VERSATILE PACIFIC SHIPYARDS, INC.

Three inventive minds created Versatile Pacific Shipyards, Inc., which is Canada's largest ship repairer and probably the country's most efficient shipbuilder.

The Victoria division, which operated for 58 years as Yarrows, owes its growth to Sir Alfred Yarrow, W. Fitzherbert Bullen, and Alfred "Andy" Wallace—plus members of their families and an array of skilled managerial, technical, and governmental helpers.

In 1893 W. Fitzherbert Bullen, who managed the Dunsmuir-owned Albion Iron Works, tried to persuade his employers to build one of the new marine railways to haul out ships. They were not interested; so, with the aid of his wife, Annie, and her brother, George Bushby, who were grandchildren of Governor Douglas, Bullen and his brother, H.F. Bullen, raised $100,000 in 1894 to start Esquimalt Marine Railway Co. It became B.C. Marine Railway, with marine ways in Esquimalt and Vancouver. It prospered in ship repair and shipbuilding.

From his new, larger shipyard at Scotstoun on the Clyde, he played a leading part in building the modern Royal Navy. He turned over his yard to war production in World War I; his 3,500 men built 29 destroyers. For these and other services, he was made a baronet.

Before World War I Alfred Yarrow was scanning the world for a strategically important place where his second son, Norman, a trained engineer, could run his own shipyard under the British flag. In 1913 he found the place he was looking for: Victoria. The Panama Canal, then under construction, should direct a steady stream of ships into the new and larger federal dry dock that had been promised for Esquimalt.

The time was right. Fitzherbert Bullen had suffered a disabling stroke, and Mrs. Bullen was ready to

From 1921 until 1946, Norman Yarrow, son of Sir Alfred Yarrow, was president and sole director of what was then Yarrows Shipyard.

sell. As a result, in 1914, Bullen's became Yarrows.

Alfred Yarrow made himself sole director and made Robert Keeay general manager, but Norman Yarrow showed his independent managerial ability. When Keeay retired in 1915, Yarrow became acting sole director. He was 24. His right-hand man, E.W. Izard, was 27.

Alfred "Andy" Wallace, the third man who was to have a major influence on Yarrows, was a shipwright from Devonshire who became a Vancouver shipbuilder at the same time that Bullen was starting up in Victoria. He built fishing boats in his backyard; then he moved to False Creek. Fishermen and cannery operators were rushing to harvest the seemingly limitless numbers of salmon. The rising market for fishing boats was his ladder to fortune. He devised a fishboat assembly line, and expanded to a new yard on Burrard Inlet, where he built larger and larger ships. His company built a floating dry dock and became Burrard Dry Dock Co.

Shipbuilding was at a low ebb between wars. The landmark events were the completion of a new 1,186-foot federal dry dock, the first automobile ferries, and the start of naval construction in Canada.

Norman Yarrow officially became sole owner in 1921. He managed the yard until the end of World War II. One of the few building contracts between wars was the wooden-hulled *Motor Princess,* the first sizable specialized automobile ferry. After the new dry dock opened in 1926, trans-Pacific Empress liners came in for overhaul and repair. Canada continued to acquire used British warships. However, in 1928 two destroyers were especially built in England for Canada, and in 1937 orders were placed for the first made-in-Canada warships. Yarrows built HMCS *Nootka,* one of four minesweepers.

Yarrows built no warships in 1914-1918, but in World War II some 3,500 workers built 5 corvettes, 17 frigates, 2 merchant ships, and 3 military transport ferries. The liner *Queen Elizabeth* was converted into an armed troopship.

Norman Yarrow sold to the Wallaces in 1946. Yarrows then became a Burrard subsidiary. Two sons of the Burrard founder took control. Clarence (later to be lieutenant-governor) was president of Yarrows, and Hubert moved to Victoria as vice-president and general manager. Later E.W. Izard and then Hubert's son John Wallace succeeded to the general manager's chair.

In the postwar years Yarrows built the 335-foot Alaska cruise steamship *Prince George,* and turned a world surplus of ships to advantage by converting oil tankers into self-dumping log barges; it helped to lead the development of "smart" self-loading, self-dumping log barges; it built tugs, barges, and ferries for inland and northern waterways. These were cut in pieces for shipment and reassem-

A navigation-aid (diesel-electric icebreaker) vessel under construction by Versatile Pacific's Victoria division for the Canadian Coast Guard.

bled on site. Aggressively searching the world for orders, Yarrows built four lighthouse tenders for France. It balanced ship business with industrial work that ranged from whaling harpoons to cathedral bells; tanks and conveyors for the lumber, paper, and mining industries; and pipes and transmission towers for hydro power.

Despite vigorous efforts to adapt and sell, however, shipyards teetered from boom to depression. The Canadian Shipbuilders and Ship Repairers' Association warned, in the 1960s, that the vital core of skilled workers was in danger of melting away. Then Canada revived its dormant naval program. The biggest projects for Yarrows were two non-magnetic minesweepers, *James Bay* and *Cowichan;* the electronic modernization of the destroyers *Sioux*

and *Algonquin;* and the building of the $25-million electronically controlled antisubmarine ship HMCS *Fraser,* which was a co-operative project divided between Burrard and Yarrows.

The naval program was innovative and experimental. Yarrows worked closely with the Navy. In 1966, however, the government changed the rules. It abandoned regional allocation of contracts to east and west, which had safeguarded plant and skilled labor in each region. It gave contracts to the lowest bidder. Western yards, with their much higher wages, received no more major naval orders. Naval building then fell into stagnation. When it resumed, B.C. yards were frozen out. The frigate program was entrusted to an eastern consortium.

Meanwhile, Yarrows had entered a new phase. In 1972 the Wallaces sold their interests. The new owner of the Victoria division of Burrard Yarrows was the Vancouver-based Cornat Corporation, which became

Versatile Cornat and then Versatile Corporation. In 1985 Burrard Yarrows was renamed Versatile Pacific Shipyards. Under the new ownership it had the added strength of a diversified corporation. A new policy of trimming bids to a lower profit margin helped secure contracts to build and enlarge B.C. ferries.

Since the 1960s B.C. yards had gained world-known expertise in building special high-technical ships: floating oceanographic laboratories, icebreaking supply ships for offshore Arctic oil fields; and patrol and service ships for fisheries protection and Coast Guard.

By the 1980s the industry faced a world surplus of ships and shipyards. Versatile Pacific Shipyards, Inc., already had some answers to that problem: greater efficiency, specialized expertise, and new products for new markets. By guaranteeing fast service, VP secured contracts to overhaul cruise ships as it had secured contracts to dry-dock supertankers 30 years earlier.

The Haida Carrier, a 340-foot, self-loading, self-dumping log barge, built by Yarrows in 1961, unloads its cargo of timber.

BRITISH COLUMBIA FERRY CORPORATION

When Premier W.A.C. Bennett drank his bedtime cup of hot ovaltine before retiring to his stateroom on the Vancouver-Victoria midnight run of the Canadian Pacific steamship *Princess Joan,* he could see that something was wrong.

The ship's cafeteria was nearly empty. Some passengers had already gone to their cabin, to sleep through the six-and-one-half-hour harbor-to-harbor voyage and go ashore in Victoria early in the morning; but the passenger load was small.

Travelling in the nearly deserted midnight boat as he moved between Victoria and his home in Kelowna during the 1950s, Premier Bennett grew aware that the age of the miniature ocean liners of the Canadian Pacific was coming to an end. They offered a high degree of passenger comfort and they had played a vital part in the development of Vancouver Island; but now people wanted to spend less time on the sea and more time in their cars. The old steamships had space for only 30 vehicles. Even the four-hour Victoria-Vancouver daytime run and the three-hour Nanaimo-Vancouver run seemed too long for impatient people.

Captain Alexander Peabody was already drawing off much of the traffic through Departure Bay, Nanaimo, to ride his Black Ball ferries, which were little more than self-propelled automobile and passenger barges.

It was a strike of ferry employees at Canadian Pacific and Black Ball in 1958 that stirred Premier Bennett to build a government-owned ferry system on the new principles of short sea distance and ample room for cars.

The provincial government took over Black Ball under emergency legislation; the federal government legislated the Canadian Pacific employees back to work; and the B.C. premier declared that never again, if he could help it, would Island-

Mainland traffic be paralyzed.

As a hardware merchant in private life, he was a self-made millionaire. Now he was ready to become an entrepreneur on behalf of the public.

He proposed to run Victoria-Vancouver ferries on a new two-hour route of only 24 nautical miles. There would be two new terminals: one at Swartz Bay, on the northern tip of the Saanich peninsula, and the other on a pod at the end of a two-mile causeway built into the sea at the nearest Mainland point, Tsawwassen. Several experts said the plan was physically and financially unworkable. No private company would risk shareholders' money to take part. Nevertheless, Premier Bennett found engineers and accountants who said it could be done; and with the help of Highways Minister P.A. "Flying Phil" Gaglardi and others, he did it.

The service started on June 15, 1960, with the 336-foot ferries *Sidney* and *Tsawwassen,* built by Victoria Machinery Depot and Burrard Dry Dock Co. (now Versatile Pacific). These ships, renamed the *Queens of Sidney* and *Tsawwassen,* were still running in 1986. They formed part of a fleet of 39 vessels serving 23 routes on the B.C. coast from Victoria to Prince Rupert. As more ships were built and more routes established or taken over, it became one of the world's largest ferry systems.

From 1960 to 1986 the number of passengers rose from 200,000 to 14 million a year. Thirty-five of the ships in the fleet of the mid-1980s, ranging from the 42-foot *Dogwood Princess II* to the 457-foot super-ferries, the *Queens of Alberni, Co-*

quitlam, Cowichan, Oak Bay, and *Surrey,* were built in British Columbia. They provided thousands of jobs as management hastened to build and enlarge ships to meet the rising demand. The number of summertime Island-Mainland sailings increased to 34 a day from each side; sea time was cut as low as 95 minutes.

"Tourism was dying on the vine here," Monty Aldous, the first general manager, who retired in Victoria, recalled in 1986. "But soon after we started, there was a boom in building hotels and motels."

Returns on money spent for the marine highway flowed back directly through the growth of population and trade. From 1960 to 1986 British Columbia's population grew from 1.6 to 2.9 million; the island kept pace, with 17 to 18 percent of the total. The ferries helped make that growth possible. Why should they make a profit, any more than roads or bridges do?

To deal with increasing traffic, greater efficiencies may be sought through new, shorter routes and money-saving techniques that yield spin-off benefits for the economy. By collaboration among B.C. Ferry Corporation, the provincial Transportation and Highways freshwater ferry fleet and private business, B.C.-designed natural-gas-propulsion, fuel-conservation, and ferry-building technologies are being developed to be sold worldwide.

Queen of Victoria moves through Active Pass on a one-hour, 35-minute Swartz Bay-Tsawwassen journey. At the end of Expo 1986, B.C. Ferries' green and white dogwood logo was to return to the ship's funnels.

FALKINS McINTOSH REED STENHOUSE

Since the discovery of gold in the 1850s, which hastened the transformation of a Hudson's Bay fur-trading post to a city, Victoria's growth and change has occurred in response to the changes within its business community. More than a century later accelerated business growth was occurring once again. Companies were enlarging their facilities, even investing in Saanich branch offices. The development of wider markets became more intense; products and services became more diversified.

One of the seldom-appreciated effects of business development is the necessity to restructure insurance protection. New equipment, products, and plants involve new—and sometimes greater—risks for owners.

During the 1960s, at Victoria's major insurance agency, two well-known commercial insurance specialists were working overtime to accommodate their fast-moving clients' needs for more comprehensive coverages. Michael Falkins and Stewart McIntosh concluded that the time was right to provide a wider range of insurance services under their own names. The doors of Falkins McIntosh were opened on May 24, 1977.

The first offices were modest; the staff was small. However, four years (and one office relocation) later, both partners realized that many of their clients—logging operations, construction contractors, manufacturers, and government agencies—required even more specialized services. Many of these companies boasted histories that began not long after the city was first incorporated. Meeting their new changes and challenges meant doing something more than merely expanding the Falkins McIntosh offices.

At the same time Reed Stenhouse,

Michael J. Falkins

Canada's largest insurance brokerage firm, had expansion plans of its own. The resulting merger made Falkins McIntosh the Vancouver Island representative of one of the world's leading insurance and reinsurance brokerage and risk management organizations.

The Falkins McIntosh Reed Stenhouse combination meant an even broader range of insurance service—services made possible by Reed Stenhouse's international scope and experience. The firm is represented in more than 30 countries, offering its sophisticated coverages and global purchasing power to an increasingly diversified group of clients.

The home of Falkins McIntosh Reed Stenhouse on 1803 Douglas Street.

Stewart McIntosh

The Reed Stenhouse corporate policy of regional autonomy is an important factor for both Falkins McIntosh and its local clients.

"We're still very much our own bosses," Mike Falkins explained at the time. "That's one of the things about the merger that appealed to us so much. It really made sense. . . .We know and understand the island."

Four years later the company acquired the commercial portfolio of Harbord Insurance, which enlarged the client base by an additional 1,200 organizations. In early 1986 new, expanded Falkins McIntosh Reed Stenhouse facilities were located within Victoria's most prestigious commercial complex, 1803 Douglas.

Growth and change—no phrase better describes the relatively short history of Falkins McIntosh Reed Stenhouse. And yet, one thing has not changed: the desire to provide service. Falkins McIntosh Reed Stenhouse is proud to provide its brokerage services to some of Vancouver Island's oldest corporations, proud to share in their heritage and be a part of their future.

—Rich Mole

DATATECH SYSTEMS, LTD.

The roots of Datatech Systems, Ltd., go back to a time when the computer had not yet found general acceptance as a commercial tool.

It was 1963 when Earl W. Large and Walter F. Large, both chartered accountants, decided to start Victoria's first computer service bureau. "We had a chartered accountancy practice we had started a year earlier," explains Earl, " and had difficulty getting work since we were not allowed to advertise or solicit business. We had started our practice with $750 a month in revenue and were looking for ways to get a competitive, innovative edge over long-established firms that had all the work. So Walter and I started the data-processing company. Back then it was new, revoluntionary."

Robert D. Ferguson, who was to become a longtime supporter and director, introduced Dr. Ted Link, a retired chief geologist from Imperial Oil Ltd. who decided to take a chance and provide critical financial assistance. The other necessary ingredient, technical capability, was obtained when Ronald B. Smith, an engineer and computer specialist, threw in his lot with the Larges.

That was the 1963 beginning of the Victoria-based nationwide data-processing, computer sales, and engineering service firm that is now listed on the Toronto and Vancouver stock exchanges as Datatech Systems Ltd. under the abbreviated label of "DTK."

"It didn't take long for the business community to realize that we could help them a great deal. For example, we ended up with many of the builders in the city using our data centre, because computerized accounting helped them identify the profitable area much better than the old hand-written reports. We expanded our expertise into most accounting areas and eventually provided service to every facet of business and gov-

As chief financial officer, Walter Large was always planning for the seeming endless expansions undertaken by the company.

ernment.

"In 1969 we went public, sold our chartered accountancy practice, obtained underwriting money, and started to expand Datatech—first with a Vancouver branch, then a Kelowna branch. At present we have 15 branches including Calgary, Ottawa, Edmonton, Winnipeg, Toronto, Kitchener, and Montreal."

Two key principles that enable Datatech to prosper in both good and bad times are careful attention to customer service and readiness to adapt to new market circumstances and technical and social change.

Earl Large (centre) supervises the arrival of the "Capital City's" first data centre computer in 1963.

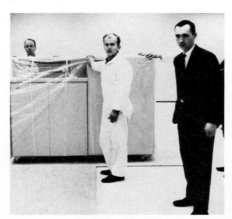

"We don't manufacture, but we decided that we should be able to repair the computers we sell, rather than let the manufacturer do it. We now service a wide variety of computers and peripherals right across Canada, and are the largest independent company offering diversified computer engineering services."

The company began with Earl and Walter Large, Ron Smith, and one employee. It now has a staff of almost 200. Marge Leisch, initially a key-puncher, was the first employee. She later became manager of the Kelowna branch. In 1986 she was the firm's semi-retired goodwill ambassador and helper.

Engineer Ron Smith, the programming specialist, is now president; Walter Large is chief financial officer; and Earl Large is chairman of the board. The head office is still in Victoria, with key regional centres in Vancouver and Toronto.

Earl Large, although born in Toronto, belongs to a long-established Victoria family and lives in a century-old house on Rockland Avenue. Business planning among flowers and trees? He explains, "It may not be for everyone, but our company is at a crossroads. We're on the verge of expanding again, and some of our best planning has come out of this environment. I love it."

"Our first expansion was to our own building in 1969 on a corner of the old Borden property at 1095 McKenzie." Mayor Hugh Curtis (right) officially congratulates Earl Large (left) as Ron Smith (centre) looks on.

CANADIAN PACIFIC

Canadian Pacific's part in shaping modern Vancouver Island is the far-western chapter of a nation-building story.

The transcontinental railway that bound together diverse territories from sea to sea had far-reaching effects on all sections of the former Crown Colony of British Columbia—including Vancouver Island, which had once been a separate colony.

Some of the early effects on Vancouver Island were negative. The engineers' choice of the Fraser River and Burrard Inlet route for the Canadian Pacific Railway (rather than Bute Inlet and a bridge to Vancouver Island) created the future metropolis of Vancouver and deprived Victoria of its older commercial supremacy. Yet Canadian Pacific played a leading part in building the economy of Vancouver Island as well; and the gains in population and income overshadowed the losses.

The island's Esquimalt and Nanaimo (E and N) Railway was built partly as a compensation to Victoria for the loss of transcontinental terminal status. Coal industrialist Robert Dunsmuir built the railway. Sir John A. Macdonald, Prime Minister of Canada, drove the last spike at Cliffside, Mile 25, on August 13, 1886.

Canadian Pacific purchased the E and N in 1905, and later extended the lines to Courtenay, Port Alberni, and Cowichan Lake.

The E and N formed part of a worldwide transportation network. Other components included the transcontinental railway line; the ships of the B.C. Coast Steamship Service; the transpacific *Empress* liners that brought passengers, tea, and silk from the Orient to Victoria and Vancouver, from which points people and cargo were relayed east and south by rail and sea; and a coast-to-coast hotel chain.

Canadian Pacific's Empress Hotel at 791 Government Street, built on

Canadian Pacific's Empress Hotel, viewed in the framework of hanging flower baskets from the south side of Victoria's Inner Harbour. The causeway and wall in front of the hotel are located in space once occupied by the wooden bridge spanning tidal James Bay. The hotel is built on landfill above former tidal mud flats.

filled-in James Bay tidal land in the downtown core of Victoria, was the last link in the hotel chain. Designed by F.M. Rattenbury, the architect of the legislative buildings, it took four years to build at a cost of $750,000. The opening of the Empress—with accompanying long-distance and regional transportation lines—made possible the growth of the tourist trade, which now provides a major

Canadian Pacific's Esquimalt and Nanaimo Railway passenger train, drawn by steam locomotive, arrives at the Cameron Lake station on the Port Alberni line about 1920.

part of Vancouver Island's income.

The Empress has hosted some seven million people, including Hollywood celebrities, the Prince of Wales (who became King Edward VIII), Prince Bernhardt of the Netherlands, the King of Siam, the Duke of Kent, the Duke of Edinburgh, Princess Margaret, King George VI, and Queen Elizabeth.

A $5-million major renovation, "Operation Teacup," was undertaken in 1966. The proposed building of a $26-million convention centre on a site originally occupied by The Empress Gardens will add a new dimension to the hotel's history.

As Canadian Pacific changed its focus and adapted to new markets and new technologies, its Pacific fleet was phased out and a cross-Canada airline came into being with routes around the world. Canadian Pacific Airlines Ltd. now flies to Victoria through a link with Air B.C.

In its early years Canadian Pacific's E and N Railway carried large amounts of Vancouver Island coal to market. Today its most important freight is lumber, pulp, and paper. Via Rail Canada provides daily passenger service over the E and N by means of the "Dayliner," which runs between Victoria and Courtenay.

Canadian Pacific's forest subsidiary, CIP Inc., manages a pulp mill, two sawmills, three logging operations, and a tree farm near Victoria, to supply the young seedlings needed for reforestation.

SWIFTSURE DEVELOPMENTS, LTD.

How did Swiftsure Developments, Ltd., score a brilliant marketing success with its country club residential communities for retired people, at a time when many other developers were either at a standstill or going broke?

Swiftsure's eye-catching triangular head office building at the end of Short Street, overlooking the southbound lane of the Blanshard Street highway extension near Saanich Road, gives a clue to the thinking of a pair of entrepreneurs who have written a new chapter in real estate history.

James Seymour Duncan and Tony Young noticed that there was an odd-shape slice of land left over from the land acquisition program that went along with the Blanshard Street widening. Nobody had bothered with this orphan fragment of rocky terrain because it seemed too cramped and crotchety to build a house on.

Young and Duncan bought it for a low price and had it re-zoned commercial, which was reasonable; McDonald's and other businesses are just around the corner. Then they built the unorthodox Swiftsure building to fit the space, commanding a wide view of city, Juan de Fuca Strait, and Olympics.

The process by which they built their head office points toward some of the basic Swiftsure operating principles: Seek out undervalued properties and disguised opportunities that everyone else has overlooked; do your market homework to be sure that the place, method, and timing are right; then launch into the project and make a thorough job of it.

That was the system they followed when they built Twin Oaks Village at Sidney and Water's Edge Village on Saanichton Bay, two town house communities for people over 45, with their own clubhouses, recreational facilities ranging from pool room to saunas and putting greens, and guest

Tony Young and Jim Duncan (from left), founder of Swiftsure Developments Ltd. Photo by Nick Boulin

rooms where visitors can stay.

When they built the first of these developments, Twin Oaks, experienced observers said they were doing it all wrong. The wrong time, because it was 1984, and the real estate market was depressed. The wrong place, near the airport, next to an industrial area and a highway.

They had heard the same kind of talk when they embarked on their first major project after organizing Swiftsure in 1976. That project was a 50-house single-family development at Sooke. However, Duncan, a native of Sooke, had a feeling for the currents of growth and change in his old home community, and the firm sold all the houses at a good profit.

When Duncan and Young planned the retirement communities, they ignored the negative talk and did some target marketing research to find out what senior citizens really wanted, and how good the chances really were. They discovered that there

were many senior citizens in the United States and other parts of Canada who were interested in retiring in Victoria. They wanted country club living with built-in space and equipment for having fun, and they wanted gardening and home repairs done for them. The location was also important—near stores, marinas, and a golf course; and handy to the airport and the ferries.

Armed with this and other market information that showed how the project could succeed, they went in search of financing. The initial response was so gloomy that they went out of town for money, and got it readily.

Young and Duncan, having made sure of their market, built the project that the critics had said was all wrong. They spent generously on an aggressive marketing campaign under the supervision of marketing director Norm Eden, and sold all 92 units within a year—far ahead of schedule.

Soon Swiftsure was launched into an even more ambitious town house retirement community, Water's Edge

Village, located on the Saanichton waterfront. It had a fenced-in security system; a clubhouse with an indoor swimming pool, jacuzzis, and saunas; a ceramic and woodworking shop; a practice putting green; a recreational vehicle storage area; and its own shuttle bus. By late summer 1986, 70 units had been completed, and the second phase was under construction. Response to the marketing campaign indicated another success.

The paths taken by Duncan and Young before becoming partners in Swiftsure Developments, Ltd., help explain the success of this unique enterprise.

Duncan absorbed the ideas and techniques of residential building development from his parents, grandparents, and uncles. His late father, Jim Duncan Senior, was a dairy and beef farmer and logger. He bought land, logged, and resold it. He taught son Jim carpentry and, sensing that the old rural Sooke would soon change under the pressure of suburban population growth, he encouraged his son to buy and sell land while he was still in his teens.

After a varied career as apprentice meat cutter, travelling attendant to prize Aberdeen Angus cattle, and gravel truck driver for Wickheim Sand and Gravel and Butler Brothers, Duncan decided, in 1973, to go into business for himself. With a partner, Larry Alexander, he built a house on speculation on Church Road—the first "spec" house in Sooke. Building lots were selling as low as $1,500. They built the entire house, from foundation to kitchen cabinets, and sold it for $29,900. At that time real estate was beginning its spectacular rise. Lots were to rise as high as $40,000, and drop down again to $18,000.

Duncan rode the escalator upward, building and selling individual residences as well as large groups of houses at increasingly high prices,

while also taking on contracts to renovate other people's houses in order to maintain the cash flow.

He subdivided, serviced, and rezoned what was left of the family farm in Sooke, sold it to a Nanaimo developer, and moved to Victoria to live. He and Tony Young met when they were working on adjoining town house developments on Ontario Street, which they successfully completed together. Together they bought and subdivided land and completed many Victoria-area subdivisions.

Young is a former carpenter's apprentice who came to Alberta in 1952, worked in construction, and then attended the University of British Columbia and studied commerce.

Swiftsure Developments' triangular building symbolized the real estate development firm's innovative approach. Photo by Nick Boulin

He and Duncan started and later expanded Swiftsure Developments, which now has sales of seven million dollars per year, and directly and indirectly employs between 50 and 100 people.

Swiftsure weathered the real estate depression by putting aside cash reserves during the good times, by cutting prices promptly and selling fast when the market turned down, by keeping costs under control, and by aggressive marketing. One of their cost-control devices is to farm out most of their construction to subcontractors, under the supervision of construction boss Lou Boujosto.

Duncan and Young talk freely about their formula for developing retirement communities. Aren't they afraid someone will copy it? "Not at all," says Young. "By the time they do, we will have moved on to something else."

CRAIGDARROCH CASTLE

Craigdarroch Castle is Victoria's most conspicuous heritage landmark. Its turrets and chimneys rise above the trees of Fort Street and appear to float in the sky like a Walt Disney vision.

Most of the 100,000 people who walk through the oak-panelled entrance hall each year are tourists who have heard that the ornate nineteenth-century mansion is an architectural treasure. Local residents tend to ignore Craigdarroch; they can always visit it some day, and they are familiar with its legend.

A poor Scottish miner persuaded his bride to travel with him to remote Vancouver Island on the promise that he would make his fortune and build her a castle. After a long search he became a millionaire almost overnight when he found a big vein of high-quality coal; so he kept his promise and built the castle.

That version is fairy-tale fiction, but the real story is just as exciting as the often-repeated folklore.

Robert Dunsmuir built the 39-room house in 1887-1889 and gave it a name that means "rocky oak place" in Gaelic. He was not a pick-and-shovel miner, but came from a family of coal masters—middle-class people who rented mines from Scotland's landowning aristocracy and gentry. He and his uncle, Boyd Gilmour, arrived in colonial Vancouver Island in 1851 to be Hudson's Bay Company's coal mine overseers and prospectors.

Dunsmuir was accompanied on the six-month voyage by his wife, Joan, and two daughters. There is no record that he promised her a castle. Their first son, James, was born en route at Fort Vancouver, which is now Vancouver, Washington.

After he had left the Hudson's Bay Company and had started prospecting on his own, Dunsmuir did in fact find a good seam of coal near Nanaimo; but he was only one of several coal discoverers and mine operators. He did not become rich overnight; it took him many years. He made his money by superior business skill, a talent for earning friendship and respect, and a shrewd political sense.

The entrepreneur recruited three Royal Navy friends to put up $27,000 for mine machinery and labor. One of them, Lieutenant Wadham Neston Diggle, invested $5,000. Dunsmuir acquired his interest 12 years later for $600,000. The exploding population of San Francisco and the increasing number of Royal Navy ships provided the market for Nanaimo coal. The growth of that market, efficiently served by Dunsmuir, Diggle and Co., was Dunsmuir's staircase to fortune.

Dunsmuir moved to Victoria, sat in the legislature for Nanaimo, and made the deals. Victoria's business leaders wanted a Vancouver Island railway. Dunsmuir was a man who got things done. As a result, the government paid him and a group of associates $750,000 in public money and 1.9 million acres of public lands, with timber and minerals, to build

---

Craigdarroch Castle, built by coal industrialist Robert Dunsmuir, looked like this at the turn of the century. The neatly tended roads, lawns, and granite walls of Craigdarroch contrast with wooden sidewalks, rough streets, and unkempt public area. The grounds were later subdivided and sold for houses. Courtesy, Provincial Archives of British Columbia, catalogue no. 5445

and take ownership of 78 miles of Esquimalt and Nanaimo Railway—which carried Dunsmuir coal to market.

Soon after the last spike had been driven, he gave orders for Craigdarroch. He was sending a status signal to the world. In the language of architecture and landscape, his sandstone mansion on a hill overlooking Victoria—surrounded by 28 acres of gardens and enclosed within a granite wall with iron gates—announced that Dunsmuir was the richest and most powerful man in British Columbia.

However, he never lived in the castle. He died just before it was finished. Joan Dunsmuir, with three of her daughters who then remained unmarried, moved into Craigdarroch in 1890 and lived there until her death in 1908. Son James built his own castle, three times larger, at Hatley Park. He became premier and then lieutenant-governor. He expanded and finally sold the family-owned empire of mines, sawmills, ironworks, ships, and railway.

After Joan's death Craigdarroch was stripped of its contents; the grounds were subdivided and sold, and the castle itself was disposed of by lottery. Too costly for a private individual to maintain, it became successively a soldiers' hospital, the seat of Victoria College, Victoria School Board, and Victoria Conservatory of Music, and a heritage-house museum owned by the city and managed by Craigdarroch Castle Historical Museum Society.

James K. Nesbitt, newspaperman and local historian, founded The Castle Society in 1959 and saved the structure from possible demolition. The 20,000-square-foot building is internationally famous as one of North America's bonanza castles, built by a man who grew wealthy by the industrial transformation of a continent.

KING BROS. LIMITED

Victoria's cargo traffic has changed beyond recognition since 1911, but the same people-skill and document-sense are still needed at King Bros. Limited, Customs Brokers and Steamship Agents.

The firm's job is to steer cargoes through customs and do all the shore housekeeping, shopping, and arranging for ships that call at Victoria and Cowichan Bay.

Edward H. King, a former clerk with Wilson Bros., one of British Columbia's largest wholesale grocery firms, founded the business in 1911 and brought in his brother Henry as a partner. Cecil Ridout started as an office boy for the firm in 1922 at the age of 15. "You may not be with us long," his employer said, "but you will meet a lot of people."

By 1986, at age 79, he is still with King Bros. as its president, while the two younger of his four sons, Lorne and Paul, manage most of the day-to-day operations. His old employer made one accurate forecast: He now has hundreds of friends and acquaintances worldwide.

As his sons take over more of the executive load, he continues to work at the public relations jobs, being dinner host with his wife, Rita, to ships' officers, solving special problems with knowledge drawn from his experience.

Knowledge is the stock-in-trade of the Ridouts: knowledge of ships, cargoes, commerce, government departments, and the thousands of items in a three-inch-thick book printed in small type, entitled *McGoldrick's Canadian Customs and Excise Tariffs.*

Cec Ridout soaked up that kind of knowledge when he worked for Edward King, who had lost a leg in World War I, and his brother Henry, whose lungs had been seared by chlorine in an industrial accident. He did most of the running and driving for both of them, so he learned fast.

From left to right: Lorne Ridout, manager; Cecil Ridout, president; Paul Ridout, operations manager.

He drove ships' captains around, delivered documents, and boarded ships at anchor with ship's papers tucked under his vest, leaving two hands free for climbing the rope ladder. He was soon promoted from messenger to ship agent.

After 22 years' service, Cec Ridout became manager when the founders retired in 1944. The firm started business upstairs at 1010 Langley Street, and moved three times before settling in its present fourth-floor offices at 1208 Wharf Street.

As Consul for Norway, Cec Ridout helped Norwegian citizens cope with emergencies and meet bureaucratic requirements; as sub-agent for Lloyd's of London, he surveyed inbound cargoes, including thousands of Austin and Hillman cars and the first shipment of Japanese motorcycles, which were damaged in transit; and in his customs broker's and ship agent's position, he kept track of a changing mercantile scene.

Before the changeover to containerships and bulk carriers concentrated the sea traffic in Vancouver area, and before the coming of an efficient highway system, large volumes of marine cargo flowed through Victoria: inbound, talc for paint-making, walnut shells for explosives filler in the James Island factory; newsreel films from the Orient, which Cec Ridout carried to the flying boat which rushed them to Seattle; out-

bound, in Prohibition days, liquor from Victoria warehouses, which was lawfully exported from Canada, documented in Mexico, and unlawfully relayed to California; lumber; Albert Head gravel for building the highways of the Olympic Peninsula; and in both directions, general cargo carried by ships of the Furness-Withy, NYK, Donaldson, Admiral, Kinglsey, and other steamship lines.

At the peak, King Bros. employed 17 people and handled an average of one ship a day. Now there is a staff of 10 and ships come once in five days, including freighters and cruise vessels. Most import cargoes now arrive by truck and air. They include electronic and plastic components for Victoria factories and china and woollens for the tourist trade. Computers are cutting down the paperwork on the interface between commerce and bureaucracy. The work has changed in detail, but its volume is steady and its basic nature is the same as it was 60 years ago.

Knowledge and human-relations skills remain today the most important parts of the business. The younger Ridouts, Lorne and Paul, say they owe their competence in these spheres to the advice and example of their father.

BAPCO: A PARTNERSHIP OF C-I-L INC. AND THE SHERWIN-WILLIAMS CO.

The British loyalty of a pioneer Victoria industrialist is remembered in the paint-manufacturing name of BAPCO.

The industrialist was William Joseph Pendray, an Englishman from Cornwall who made a fortune from gold, soap, and paint. He chose the name of British America Paint Company for his paint factory.

This title was shortened to BAPCO; and the Victoria-based enterprise was owned and managed by three generations of Pendrays before it was sold to what was then Canadian Industries Ltd.

For people of the 1980s, the British America title carried an echo of the days when transplanted British immigrants brought the Union Jack with them and referred to Britain as "home."

However, the Victoria where the BAPCO story began was a more cosmopolitan place than the often-heard "little-bit-of-old-England" stereotype implies; and although British frontier adventurers such as William J. Pendray maintained a reference point in Britain, their commercial vision was worldwide. Pendray's hopes of fortune caused him to reach out to British Columbia, the western United States, and South Africa.

He was born in 1846 in St. Just, Cornwall. When he was a young man, reports of North American gold drew him across the Atlantic, over the Isthmus of Panama by wagon, by ship to San Francisco, and from there to the mines at Grass Valley, Nevada.

After eight months of work as a hired hand at three dollars a day, he left for what he saw as a more promising gold field under the Union Jack in the Cariboo district of the Crown Colony of British Columbia.

According to Pendray family records, he struck it rich in 1867 at his claim on Mosquito Creek; and after he had accumulated a sizable amount

The old BAPCO paint factory on Laurel Point, which has since been replaced by a hotel complex. Photo was taken circa 1950. Courtesy, Victoria City Archives

of gold, he decided to return to England. After he returned to England, he is said to have invested his fortune in South African gold mines, and lost it all.

During a three-month stay in England he met and wished to marry Amelia Jane Carthew. However, he needed money to support a wife in comfortable style, so he set out for North America again in the hope of making another fortune.

Family records say he made enough money in the mines of Virginia City, Nevada, to move back to Victoria with the aim of starting a business. He was a British loyalist. The Union Jack flew over that small city of British, U.S., and Canadian immigrants and their first-generation offspring; and the prospect of spectacular population growth after the completion of a transcontinental railway had a special meaning for a commercial entrepreneur.

William J. Pendray's uncle, W.J. Jeffree, was already established in Victoria as a clothing merchant, and Pendray had a standing invitation to join the firm; but he declined. He

wanted his own business. He took his time and kept scouting the town for promising opportunities.

When he was rambling among the buildings that line the shore of tidal James Bay, he found a small soap factory that had been vacant since the death of its owner. This might be the opportunity he had been looking for.

His venture did so well that in 1876 he was able to move to a much larger building just inside James Bay bridge. By the following year the staff of two had increased to 45 employees making a variety of soaps, including two kinds of whale oil soap for insect-killing and household use; white, blue, brown, and mottled household soap; and three kinds of

W.J. Pendray's first soap factory on James Bay waterfront. Courtesy, Victoria City Archives

toilet soap: carbolic, shaving, and glycerine, as well as other house and garden products.

He was now prosperous enough to send to England for his fiancee, Amelia. They were married in 1877, and they went to live on Douglas Street at the corner of Kane Street, now known as Broughton Street. They had a small cottage commanding a view of the wooden sidewalks and the chain gangs of convicts passing by on their way to work on the muddy streets.

The Pendrays had four sons: Ernest, Carl, Herbert, and Roy. When the eldest sons were born, the prudent William Pendray started looking for another way to secure their future. He wanted to launch another enterprise that had the potential to grow and prosper. He settled on the paint business.

He bought the factory of the Canada Paint Co. on Store Street north of the Johnson Street bridge, renamed it the British America Paint Co., and went into production.

In its first years the soap factory had to subsidize the paint factory, but sales and profits rose steadily until the paint factory ran out of space, and Carl Pendray bought a new and larger site at Laurel Point in 1890.

The Pendray mansion on Belleville Street, built in 1897, is now a restaurant. Courtesy, Victoria City Archives

He wanted to live near the factory, so he commissioned architect Thomas Hooper to build him a mansion on the Inner Harbour. It was an ornate three-storey house with pepperpot turret, wide verandas, and an interior glowing with oak panelling, ceiling paintings by Muller and Sturn, and many-coloured windows that had been brought by ship from

The first soap factory operated by the founder of BAPCO Paint is the tall white building just the other side of the old James Bay bridge. Courtesy, Victoria City Archives

Venice around Cape Horn packed in molasses. There also was plenty of space for children to play in the grounds and the big attic.

By 1906 his son Ernest was foreman in the soap factory; J. Carl (who was destined to become mayor of Victoria) was manager of the paint factory; and Herbert was paint foreman. The paint factory was self-contained; it printed its own labels and made its own cans in its own tin shop. It had its own box factory where it made wooden boxes for shipping cans of paint and also turned out cardboard boxes for sale.

Big changes were about to happen. The soap business was sold to Lord Leverhulme and amalgamated with his Sunlight Soap Company. No more soap was made in Victoria. The lands surrounding the factory, out into the muddy flats, were sold to Canadian Pacific to make the site for the Empress Hotel. The paint works prospered and began to ship all over the West; but in 1913 William Pendray was killed when the feed pipe on a new water tank broke loose and struck him.

The founder's eldest surviving son, J. Carl Pendray, became president, and he was succeeded in 1948 by his son, Allan. The BAPCO plant grew to be the largest west of Toronto and north of San Francisco. The firm had retail outlets throughout the West and another factory in Winnipeg.

In 1965 the company was sold to C-I-L, which moved the factory away from Victoria. The Laurel Point site was turned over to a $20-million hotel and apartment complex.

The historic BAPCO name now symbolizes the C-I-L-Sherwin-Williams partnership which markets paint Canada-wide. From a distribution centre in Surrey, British Columbia, the successor to the Pendray enterprises sells paint under C-I-L's Cilux label and Sherwin-Williams' Kem label.

CREASE & COMPANY

Construction watchers at the corner of Douglas and Fort streets on a spring day in 1964 saw a massive desk being manoeuvred with a crane into the unfinished, skeletal eighth floor of the Bentall Building.

The seven- by four-foot desk was part of the history of Crease & Company, the law firm that was then preparing to move into this building from its old location in Bastion Square. Crease & Company had been formed by an amalgamation of four long-established firms and the heirloom desk had belonged to Sir Lyman Poore Duff, Chief Justice of the Supreme Court of Canada, when he was a young lawyer practising in Victoria with one of the component firms, then known as Bodwell, Duff and Irving. The desk would be too big to go through windows and doors, so it was lifted into place before the glass was fitted.

The namesake beginning of Crease & Company was a practice founded in 1891 by Lindley Crease, son of Sir Henry Pering Pellew Crease, the first practising barrister on Vancouver Island. Henry Crease became attorney-general and later a judge of the Supreme Court of British Columbia. Lindley joined with his brother Arthur and Frederick C. Fowkes under the name of Crease and Crease. This firm and three others, founded in 1879, 1885, and 1914, amalgamated as Crease & Company.

One of the senior partners now has Duff's desk. Its changed use illustrates the changes in law and society during the Crease firm's more than 100 years of practice. In the nine-

Sir Lyman Poore Duff, chief justice of the Supreme Court of Canada. Before Duff became a judge of the Supreme Court in 1904, he practised law as a member of the firm of Bodwell, Irving & Duff. Courtesy, Provincial Archives of British Columbia, Catalogue No. 5435

teenth century that desk accommodated two lawyers, one on each side. It was a "partnership desk," with a place for a lawyer on each side in the leisurely days when lawyers were general practitioners and could conveniently share a small space. In the busier, specialized, and more impersonal 1980s, more phoning and greater concentration require separate offices.

"Twenty years ago Crease & Company would have had a couple of dozen full-fledged trials a year," Lyman Robinson, University of Victoria law professor and former dean, said after spending a year with the

Arthur Crease (left) and Lindley Crease— September 1901. Courtesy, Provincial Archives of British Columbia, Catalogue No. 11860

firm as academic in residence. "Now there are four or five people doing counsel work, each handling several dozen trials a year."

Greater numbers of laws and more public awareness of law are among reasons for the increased work load. Laws and regulations have mushroomed. Annual volumes of statutes and regulations increased threefold from the 1960s to 1980s. Television focussed attention on the law, and spurred more people to pursue their interests in court, or in the new quasi-judicial tribunals.

In 1986 the firm had 14 lawyers, each with special fields of expertise; two senior retired partners, one of whom was still associate counsel; two articled students; plus paralegal assistants and 22 office and administrative staff. D.J. Lawson is the retired partner no longer in practice. J.C. Scott-Harston, retired partner and associate counsel, is author of a legal textbook, *Tax Planned Will Precedents*. The partners in 1986 were R.N. Samson, R. Lou-Poy, J.D. Patterson, P.W. Klassen, R.T. Taylor, G.C. Whitman, J.E.D. Savage, and J.K. Greenwood.

By 1986 the firm had a tradition of political detachment; yet two of its ancestral firms produced B.C. premiers, the brothers A.E.B. Davie and Theodore Davie, who founded Davie & Pooley and Davie & Bodwell, respectively. Each Davie was also attorney-general. The Pooley firm contributed another attorney-general, R.H. Pooley.

Davie & Bodwell became Bodwell, Irving & Duff, then Bodwell & Lawson. Davie & Pooley became Pooley & Davie. The youngest ancestral firm began with Harold R. Beckwith, who joined with the future Mr. Justice H.W. Davey of B.C. Court of Appeal in a firm that became Davey and Baker. Amalgamations of the four legal "lineages" created Crease & Company.

STENNER FINANCIAL SERVICES LTD.

Steering people to financial security in a dangerous world is the task of Stenner Financial Services Ltd., a British Columbia-based investment and financial planning company.

Gordon V. Stenner, president and founder, says guidance by wise, skilled, and sensitive financial planners is much needed at this time of global economic change.

In 1986 Stenner, with the aid of 100 financial planners, research, and support staff, was co-ordinating the care of $250 million of other people's money from the firm's head office in the old city hall on the main street, Abbotsford. The total investment was increasing at the rate of about $100 million a year. There were 21 offices in British Columbia including six on Vancouver Island, with new branches being considered nationally. Stenner's 20,000 investors ranged from the trustees of multimillion-dollar pension funds to small wage earners who were putting away $100 a month.

Because of the new socio-economic tides that are scouring the world in the last years of the twentieth century, Stenner believes that the chances to accumulate wealth as well as the chances to lose everything and go disastrously broke are greater than ever before. These unprecedented social forces include soaring world population, alternating inflation and deflation in some countries, heavy international debt loads and government deficits, fluctuating energy prices, the rapid march of invention and technological change, the industrialization of some Third World countries, and upheavals in the economies of traditional industrial nations.

At the same time some direction-finding and control devices have come into being to enable people to prosper exceedingly in changing conditions. They include mutual funds, which allow people of relatively small means as well as big investors to hire professional investment managers who act on their behalf to build up portfolios of holdings in which gains consistently out-perform losses; an increasingly accurate and detailed world network of rapidly transmitted economic information; and a sharpened capacity for fast, thorough, and precise computer analysis and insightful, hands-on appraisal of the performance of business enterprises.

In the course of a career in financial planning and investment that began in 1963, Stenner developed a strategy for applying modern techniques of analysis, plus friendly personal care, to give each client a financial plan tailored to his individual needs and wishes.

During the early years of his career Stenner was a successful representative of a national firm offering financial plans. However, he began to feel that he was not doing the best possible job for his clients. For four years he dropped out of the financial world and followed his deep religious faith, becoming a Free Methodist pastor. In 1970, after a near-fatal automobile accident, he returned to financial planning as a representative of the largest firm of its kind in Canada, and became the first person to break the $10-million barrier in volume of plans implemented—a feat the president of the company likened to running the four-minute mile.

Privately, he continued to develop his own financial planning concept, but the rules did not let him put it to

On Vancouver's False Creek waterfront, Gordon V. Stenner poses with a wood-carved helmsman—a symbolic representation of the Stenner Financial Services ideal of setting a calculated course for financial security.

work. As a result, he started his own company. The first office opened in Clearbrook, next to Abbotsford, in February 1984. During the years of alternating expansion and consolidation that followed, he travelled the country and the world, interviewing investment managers, recruiting planners, opening offices, writing financial articles and columns, and making over 100 local and national television and radio appearances annually.

At Stenner Financial Services Ltd., wishes and hopes of the client are tested through an in-depth interview; the client's investment bias is classified on a 10-point risk-scale from ultra-conservative to ultra-aggressive; and an individual personal financial plan is drawn up on request to give the client the degree of tax shelter, income, capital gain, and security he prefers. No fees or commission are levied without advance agreement.

Stenner analysts sift through 300 mutual funds that offer everything from bonds to common stocks, precious metals to real estate. They choose those that are best managed, and keep them under daily surveillance. They look for steady rather than erratic growth, and the firm awards the most points to investment managers who show they can see ahead rather than react to past events—those who can make money in bad times as well as good times.

"We look for maximum return with low risk, but there is no such thing as a riskless investment," Gordon Stenner says. For example, a Stenner Japanese Fund stands at 9 on the one-to-10 risk scale. It yielded 141 percent over a recent 12-month period ending August 1986. Templeton Growth Fund stands at 8. It has returned 23 percent, compounded annually; $10,000 invested in 1954 would have been worth more than $1.1 million in 1986.

CAPITAL BROADCASTING SYSTEM LIMITED

A trophy hanging on the wall tells the story of Capital Broadcasting System Limited and its founder, David M. Armstrong, in two words: public service. The oak and silver shield indicates that a jury of fellow broadcasters, weighing the record of help to humanitarian, public causes among all British Columbia radio stations, awarded first prize in 1985 to CKDA-AM 1200 and CFMS-FM Stereo 98.5.

In the same year that his stations earned that honor, David Armstrong died suddenly at the age of 65.

His policy of supporting community causes with gifts, promotional energy, and ample air time was true to his personal ethic. He often told his wife, Sheridon, that he believed in giving back good measure to the community that had treated him well. "Our strength is community (involvement), regard for news and what's happening in Victoria," David Armstrong told a reporter in 1980. "After all, music can be heard here on 50 stations."

He took a lot of trouble to give the community the kind of information service it wanted, including frequent sea reports for the thousands of boaters on Vancouver Island and Mainland shores. It was typical of David Armstrong that when he retired his own 40-foot boat, Saturna Chief, in which he and his family and executives had seen many happy times on combined business-pleasure cruises, he made a gift of the boat to the British Columbia Lifeboat Society. The Armstrong stations put their weight behind a variety of community causes, from the Steve Fonyo run for the Canadian Cancer Society to Mark Sutton's record-breaking 488-day flagpole-sitting feat for the Canadian Paraplegic Society, the Good Samaritan Fund, and also CKDA's Christmas Dream project which raises some $40,000 a year in cash and toys for underprivileged

David Armstrong (1919-1985), founder of Capital Broadcasting System Limited. P.S.D. Pears, photographer

families.

The policy of community involvement, together with a well-contrived marketing strategy and a talent for hiring and motivating good people, paid off in public respect and in profits. In 1986 CKDA was number one among Victoria's four stations in size of audience; CFMS was number one in listening hours per week.

As a teenager at Mount View High School in World War II, he sensed the market for entertainment that had been created when thousands of people were uprooted and dumped far from home. He made a good income by organizing two bands and staging dances. "He really did drive a better car than the principal," an old friend said.

He learned his trade as an announcer at Victoria Station CFCT-CJVI, and in Prince Albert; as salesman for CKMO (later CFUN), Vancouver; and as sales manager for CKNW, New Westminster. Armstrong succeeded in getting a Victoria licence on the fourth try. He put the new station on the air on January 18, 1950, at 250 watts for $100,000, of which $25,000 was his savings, $25,000 a loan from his mother, and $50,000 a bank loan. He was the right man at the right

time. "You couldn't put a station like CKDA or CFMS on the air for less than three million dollars today," Chuck Camroux, his longtime friend and consultant, said in 1986.

As early as possible he boosted his station to the maximum allowable 50,000 watts and in 1954 he secured British Columbia's first FM licence, which he did not fully activate until 1965. His hunches, and his voracious reading and listening in search of trends, paid off in success.

His CKDA, which moved from middle-of-the-road to adult contemporary in the late 1970s, holds the top rating for the young to middle-aged; CFMS, with its good music and nostalgia and its information up front, has the ear of people who are middle-aged or more.

He secured British Columbia's first low-powered TV licence for CHEK-TV in 1956 and went full power in 1960. Because he was undercapitalized, he had two choices: give up sole ownership of the radio stations or sell the TV station. He sold the TV station.

Chuck Camroux says David Armstrong was one of the last of the dedicated hands-on broadcasters in a scene already dominated by accountants and business school graduates. Until the day he died, he was still doing his own in-depth interview broadcasts. Friends say he did not want to share control of his stations. He wanted to keep them and hand them over intact to his family.

Today his widow, Sheridon, is president of the company, which operates the two stations and Golden Sound Background Music. Profits and ratings are higher than ever. She is winning a battle against a challenge to her control. Her children, Montgomery, Spencer, Gowan, and Karalyn, aged 13 to 18, are looking forward to careers in the hometown broadcasting empire their father had built for them.

Patrons

The following individuals, companies, and organizations have made a valuable commitment to the quality of this publication. Windsor Publications and the Greater Victoria Civic Archives Society gratefully acknowledge their participation in *Beyond the Island: An Illustrated History of Victoria.*

Bapco: A Partnership of C-I-L Inc. and the Sherwin-Williams Co.*
B.C. Tel*
British Columbia Ferry Corporation*
The Butchart Gardens Ltd.
Canadian Pacific*
Capital Broadcasting System Limited*
Craigdarroch Castle*
Crease & Company*
S. Joseph Cunliffe
Datatech Systems, Ltd.*
W.G. Estates
Falkins McIntosh Reed Stenhouse*
G & O Holdings Ltd.
Greater Victoria Chamber of Commerce

Dr. K. Ian Hadfield
Irish Linen Stores
Island Farms Dairy*
James Bay Tea Room & Restaurant
King Bros. Limited*
McGill and Orme, Ltd.*
Oakwood Developments: A Joint Venture of E.Y. Construction Ltd.
Pemberton, Holmes Ltd.*
Pemberton Houston Willoughby*
Simpson Drapery Ltd.
Stenner Financial Services Ltd.*
Swiftsure Developments, Ltd.*
Thorne Ernst Whinney
Times-Colonist*
Van Isle Water Services Ltd.
Versatile Pacific Shipyards, Inc.*
Victoria Book & Stationery
Victoria Fiddlesticks Ltd.
Victoria's Ogden Point Docks Operated by Westcan Terminals Ltd.*

*Partners in Progress of *Beyond the Island: An Illustrated History of Victoria.* The histories of these companies and organizations appear in Chapter VI, beginning on page 112.

BIBLIOGRAPHY

The following is a selected bibliography of the materials which proved to be the most useful in writing this book.

PRIMARY

Municipality of Saanich, Archives
Canadian Manufacturing Association, Vancouver Island Branch, 1949-1965.

National Archives & Records Services, Washington, D.C.
Victoria, B.C., Consular Port Files, 1907-1949.

Provincial Archives of British Columbia
American Consul Dispatches, Victoria, 1862-1906;
Attorney General's Papers, 1910-1939;
Colonial Office/Hudson's Bay Company, Correspondence;
Herald Street Collection;
J.D. Pemberton Journal;
Provincial Secretary's Papers, 1872-1898;
Vertical File;
Victoria City Directories.

Public Archives of Canada
Department of Agriculture, R.G. 17; Department of Labour Papers, R.G. 27;

Victoria City Archives
Annual Reports, Victoria, 1882-1975; Assessment Roles, Victoria, 1862-1891;
City Council Papers, 1862-1939; City of Victoria, Magistrate Records, 1882-1885;
City Solicitor's Papers, 1910-1955; Mayor's Papers, 1950-1975.

SECONDARY
Books
Bowsfield, H., ed. *Fort Victoria Letters, 1846-51.* Winnipeg: HBC Records Society, 1979.

Everett, T.T. *Victoria Illustrated: A Brief History of Victoria from 1842.* Victoria, 1892.

Fawcett, E. *Some Reminiscences of Old Victoria.* Toronto: William Briggs, 1912.

Fisher, R. *Contact & Conflict.* Vancouver: University of British Columbia Press, 1977.

Forward, C.N., ed. *Residential & Neighbourhood Studies in Victoria.* Victoria: University of Victoria, 1973.

Foster, H.O., ed. *Victoria: Physical Environment & Development.* Victoria: University of Victoria, 1976.

Gregson, H. *A History of Victoria, 1842-1970.* Victoria: The Victoria Observer Publishing Company, 1970.

McIntosh, Robert Dale. *A Documentary History of Music in Victoria.* Vol. I, *1850-1899.* Victoria: University of Victoria, 1981.

Mills, G.F. *Architectural Trends in Victoria, B.C., 1850-1914.* Two volumes, Ottawa: Parks Canada, 1976.

Pethick, D. *Summer of Promise, Victoria, 1864-1914.* Victoria: Sono Nis Press, 1980.

———— *Victoria, The Fort.* Vancouver: Mitchell Press, Ltd., 1968.

Reksten, T. *Rattenbury: A Victorian Architect.* Victoria: Sono Nis Press, 1978.

Segger, M. and Franklin D. *Victoria: A Primer for Regional History in Architecture, 1843-1929.* New York: The American Foundation and Study Institute, 1979.

Victoria, Corporation of the City of. *Victoria Illustrated.* Victoria, 1891.

Weddington, A. *The Fraser Mines Vindicated or The History of Four Months.* Victoria: De Gravo, 1858.

Articles
Adams, Thomas. "Town Planning in B.C.: The Example of Victoria." *Town Planning & Conversation of Life,* 4 (July 1918): 65-70.

Brook, G.W.S. "Edgar Crow Baker: An Entrepreneur in Early British Columbia." *B.C. Studies,* 31 (1976): 23-43.

Brown, T.R.G. "Crime & Disorder in Colonial Victoria, 1862." unpublished paper, Department of History, University of Victoria, 1984.

Careless, J.M.S. "The Lowe Brothers, 1852-70: A Study of Business Relations on the North Pacific Coast." *B.C. Studies,* 2 (1969): 1-18.

—— "The Business Community in the Early Development of Victoria, B.C." *Canadian Business History: Selected Readings,* (1972): 104-23.

Cary, S.H.D. "The Church of England and the Colony Question in Victoria, 1860." *Journal of the Canadian Church Historical Society,* 24 (1982): 63-74.

Cauthers, J., ed. "A Victorian Tapestry: Impressions of Life in Victoria, B.C., 1880-1914." *Sound Heritage,* 7 (1978): 1-76.

Duff, W. "The Fort Victoria Treaties." *B.C. Studies,* 3 (1969): 3-57.

Foner, P.S. "The Coloured Inhabitants of Vancouver Island." *B.C. Studies,* 8 (1970-71): 29-33.

Forward, C.N. "Relationships Between Elderly Population and Income Sources in the Urban Economic Bases of Victoria & Vancouver." *B.C. Studies,* 36 (1977-78): 34-46.

———— "The Development of Victoria as a Retirement Center." *Ur-*

ban *History Review,* 13 (1984): 117-120.

————- "The Evolution of Victoria's Functional Character." *Town & City: Aspects of Western Canadian Urban Development,* (1981): 347-370.

Grant, C. "Vancouver Island." *Royal Geographical Society,* 27 (1857): 268-320.

Lai, Chuen-Yan David. "The Chinese Consolidated Benevolent Association in Victoria: Its Origins and Functions." *B.C. Studies,* 15 (1972): 53-67.

————- "Chinese Attempts to Discourage Emigration to Canada: Some Findings from the Chinese Archives in Victoria." *B.C. Studies,* 18 (1973): 33-49.

Lamb, W.K. "The Founding of Fort Victoria." *British Columbia Historical Quarterly,* 7 (1943): 71-92.

Lutz, J. "De-Industrialization, 1890-1900." unpublished paper, Department of History, University of Victoria, 1984.

McDonald, R.A.J. "Victoria, Vancouver and the Evolution of British Columbia's Economic System, 1886-1914." *British Columbia: Historical Readings,* (1981): 369-395.

McKnight, D. "A Little Bit of Old Harry: Crime and Disorder in Victoria, 1859." *Register,* 3 (1982): 158-83.

Paterson, D.G., and J. Wilen. "Depletion and Diplomacy: The North Pacific Seal Hunt, 1886-1910." *Research in Economic History,* 2 (1977): 81-139.

Roy, P.E. "The Illumination of Victoria: Late Nineteenth Century Technology and Municipal Enterprise." *B.C. Studies,* 32 (1976-77): 79-92.

Sager, W.E. "The Shipping Industry in British Columbia, 1867-1914: A Preliminary Examination of the Vessel Registries." Paper presented to the Canadian Historical Associ-ation, Vancouver, June 1983.

Theses

Bridge, A.B. "Two Victorian Gentle-women in the Colonies of Vancouver Island and British Columbia: Eleanor Hill Fellows and Sarah Lindley Crease." Master's thesis, University of Victoria, 1984.

Gallacher, D.T. "City in Depression: The Impact of the Years 1929-1939 on Greater Victoria, B.C." Master's thesis, University of Victoria, 1969.

Floyd, P.R. "The Human Geography of South-East Vancouver Island, 1842-1891." Master's thesis, University of Victoria, 1969.

Gould, C.E.J. "Wartime Housing in Victoria, BC: Direct Federal Government Intervention in Housing and Subsequent Alterations to Standardized Designs." Master's thesis, University of Victoria, 1977.

Johnson-Draw, C.B. "The Crease Family & the Arts in Victoria B.C." Master's thesis, University of Victoria, 1980.

Lee, C.L. "The Effect of Planning Controls on the Morphology of the City of Victoria, British Columbia." Master's thesis, University of Victoria, 1969.

Lines, K. "A Bit of Old England: The Selling of Tourist Victoria." Master's thesis, University of Victoria, 1972.

McCann, L.D. "The Structure and Patterning of Manufacturing in the Victoria Metropolitan Area." Bachelor's essay, University of Victoria, 1966.

Mackie, R. "Colonial Land, Indian Labour and Company Capital: The Economy of Vancouver Island, 1849-1858." Master's thesis, University of Victoria, 1984.

Pilton, J.W. "Early Negro Settlement in Victoria." Bachelor's essay, University of British Columbia, 1949.

Robertson, I.E. "The Business Community and the Development of Victoria, 1858-1900." Master's thesis, University of Victoria, 1981.

Robertson, R.W. "The Relocation of Residents Displaced From the Rose-Blanshard Renewal Scheme in Victoria, B.C." Master's thesis, University of Victoria, 1970.

Ruzicka, S.E. "The Decline of Victoria as the Metropolitan Center of British Columbia, 1885-1901." Master's thesis, University of Victoria, 1973.

Sandberg, L.A. "A Study in Canadian Political Economy: A Critical Review and the Case of the British Columbia Salmon Canning Industry, 1870-1914." Master's thesis, University of Victoria, 1979.

Sedwick, C.P. "Context of Economic Change and Continuity in an Urban Overseas Chinese Community." Master's thesis, University of Victoria, 1973.

Sullivan, M. "Threats to the Independence of the Elderly Poor: A Study of an Inner City Hotel." Master's thesis, University of Victoria, 1981.

Thackray, W.S. "Keeping the Peace on Vancouver Island: The Colonial Police and the Royal Navy, 1850-1866." Master's thesis, University of Victoria, 1980.

Thornton, D.M. "Victoria's Relative Economic Decline: The Case of the Albion Iron Works, 1862-1910." Honours Bachelor's paper, University of Victoria, 1984.

Tozer, D.J. "State Intervention, The Community Movement and the Neighbourhood Improvement Program in James Bay, Victoria." Master's thesis, University of Victoria, 1981.

Walden, F.E. "The Social History of Victoria, B.C. 1858-1971." Bachelor's thesis, University of British Columbia, 1951.

Index